三島喜美代
――未来への記憶

MISHIMA KIMIYO
MEMORIES for the FUTURE

SEIGENSHA

CONTENTS

はじめに

このたび、練馬区立美術館では「三島喜美代―未来への記憶」展を開催いたします。

1932年、大阪に生まれた三島喜美代は、私たちの身の回りにあふれる情報やゴミを一貫したテーマとして、70年にわたる制作活動を展開してきた現代美術家です。当初はコラージュやシルクスクリーンの技法を取り入れながら絵画を描いていましたが、1970年頃からは新聞やチラシなどの印刷物を陶に転写し、焼成する立体作品へと表現方法を変え、独自のスタイルを確立しました。その作品は一見すると遊び心やユーモアにあふれていますが、過剰な情報化社会の中に埋没する危機感や恐怖感が表現され、また大量消費社会に向けて批判的なまなざしを投げかけるものとなっています。

近年、三島作品への評価が日本国内はもとより海外からも急激に高まっており、2023年には遅まきながら三島の展覧会が初めて美術館で開かれました。東京の美術館における初の個展となる本展では、陶によって再現された新聞や空き缶などのオブジェの数々、それらの作品のベースとなった初期平面作品のほか、代表作と目される巨大なインスタレーション作品《20世紀の記憶》、さらに近作を加えることによって三島の活動の全貌をたどります。「好奇心が一番大事。失敗ばかりしていたが、それが面白かった」と自身の制作について語る三島の魅力的でエネルギッシュな作品世界を、多数の観客の皆様にご堪能いただければ幸いです。

本展の開催にあたりましては、三島喜美代氏から惜しみないご助言と格別のご高配を賜りました。この場を借りて心より御礼申し上げます。また貴重な作品を快くご出品くださった美術館や所蔵家の皆様、企画段階よりご協力くださった岐阜県現代陶芸美術館、広報協力並びに出品協力をいただいた株式会社東横イン/株式会社ギャラリー1045、そして本展の実現に向けてご尽力を賜った多数の関係各位に深く感謝申し上げます。

2024年5月

練馬区立美術館

Foreword

The Nerima Art Museum is pleased to announce the opening of the exhibition "Mishima Kimiyo: Memories for the Future."

Born 1932 in Osaka, Mishima Kimiyo has been active as a contemporary artist for over 70 years, creating works that are consistently themed around the floods of information and waste that surround us in daily life. Starting off with paintings that incorporated collaging and silkscreen printing techniques, from around 1970, Mishima went on to establish her own unique style of transferring newspapers, leaflets and other printed matter, onto clay that she finished into fired ceramic items. While looking playful and full of humor on the outside, these are artworks that express the sense of crisis and fear that lies underneath the surface of today's information flood society, while projecting the artist's critical view on mass consumption society in general.

In recent years, interest and appreciation for Mishima's work has increased significantly not only in Japan but also overseas, and her first ever exhibition at an art museum was eventually shown – somewhat belatedly – in 2023. This exhibition, first solo show at a museum in Tokyo, features a number of ceramic objects imitating things like newspapers or empty beverage cans, as well as early two-dimensional works that served as a foundation for these sculptures, and *Memories of the 20th Century*, a large installation piece that is regarded as Mishima's most representative work. Several recent works complete this exhaustive introduction to the artist who says about her production manners that "curiosity has been the most important thing, and even through it resulted in one mistake after another, that was what made it all interesting." We hope that this exhibition will be an opportunity for a broad audience to experience the artist's fascinating and energetic art.

We are deeply grateful to Mishima Kimiyo for her great help and generous advice to us in organizing the exhibition. We would also like to thank the museums and collectors that willingly provided items from their precious collections; the Museum of Modern Ceramic Art, Gifu, for their cooperation from the planning stage; Toyoko Inn Co., Ltd. / Gallery 1045 for their PR and exhibition-related cooperation; and everyone else involved in the realization of this exhibition, for their invaluable support.

May 2024

Nerima Art Museum

三島喜美代の「おもろさ」

徳山拓一

三島喜美代の魅力は、あっけらかんとした気韻生動にある。ダイナミックな作品が放つ力強さは晴れ渡る青空のように突き抜けていて、観るたびに清々しい気持ちにしてくれる。同時に、それらは現代社会に向けられた批評的な眼差しに裏打ちされており、三島の作品は、普段私達が疑うことのない日常に疑義を表明し、そこに潜む脆さを剥き出しにする。しかし、そこには押し付けがましい教条主義的な主張は一切なく、ただ現実世界の有様が、そこに内在する矛盾も含めて白日の下に引きずり出されているだけなのである。

三島に制作の動機を尋ねると、「おもろそうやなーっと思ったから」という答えが返ってくる。モチーフや手法の選択の理由を聞かれても「ただ面白いと思ったから。あんまり考えてません」と言い切ることが多い。新聞紙も、ゴミ箱の空き缶も、サンキストの段ボール箱も、陶器で作ったら面白そうだと思ったから、なのだと。まさに、あっけらかんとした澱みのない動機なのである。本稿では、三島を突き動かす「おもろさ」について、それが美術の文脈においてどのように受容されてきたのか、そして、それを起点に70年以上という三島のキャリアを通してようやく全貌が見えてきたであろう、三島作品の意味について改めて考察してみたい。

*　*　*

三島喜美代は、大阪市の十三（じゅうそう）で喫茶店を営んでいた両親のもとに生まれた。高等女学校（現在の中学校）の担任が画家であったことから絵を描くことに興味を覚え、油彩を始めた。1年時に終戦を迎え、それまでの臨画中心の教育が終わり、自由な画風が許されるようになっていた。その頃の三島は、画家や芸術家ではなく、医学部に進学し研究者になりたいと考えていた。幼少期から顕微鏡を 5台も持っていた三島は、昆虫や自分の髪の毛など、いろいろなものを顕微鏡で観察して遊んでいた。[1] 研究者になって実現したかったことは、人間のクローンを製作することだったという。それを母親に話すと知り合いの医者に相談され、「人間を創るなどということは神への冒涜だ」と諭され、医学部進学の夢は断たれることになったという。女学校の卒業後は、油彩に没頭するようになり、絵画教室でのちに夫となる三島茂司（1920-1985年）と出会った。具体美術協会の吉原治良（1905-1972年）に師事していたこともある三島茂司を通じて、三島は先端の美術の動向に触れることになり、美術の道を突き進んでいくことになる。

三島の女学校の卒業の頃は1947年前後。クローン羊のドリーが生まれたのが1997年なので、その50年前に人間を創るという発想を抱いていた三島の好奇心と想像力、あるいは、先見の明には驚かされるものがある。そんな三島が本格的に絵画を始めた1950年代の関西は、まさに新しい美術表現が胎動していた時代であった。終戦直後の日本では戦争によって困窮した生活からの1日も早い復興が求められ、人々の価値観や政治経済は大きく変化し、同じように、美術界も重要な転換期を迎えていた。戦後の関西には確認できるだけでも60以上の美術団体があった。若い作家たちは、新たな時代のイデオロギーに相応しい表現を希求し、様々な動向を生み出そうとしていた。

絵を描きたいという純粋な動機から制作を始めていた三島であったが、この頃にはひとりの表現者として絵画を追求するようになったのではないだろうか。それは、画風が具象画から抽象画に変化していったことと軌を一にしているように思える。三島は、当時美術界を席巻していたアンフォルメルの影響を受けた抽象絵画を精力的に制作し、1954年から1969年まで独立美術協会に出品し、1963年に独立賞、1965年にはシェル美術賞展で佳作賞を受賞し、着実にアーティストとして歩み始めていた。三島は特定の美術団体に属することはなかったが、戦後の関西に醸成されていた新しい表現を欲する熱量の中で、独自の表現言語、あるいは、「おもろい」表現を探求していたはずである。それは夢中になって顕微鏡を覗き込んでいた幼少期の姿に重なる。

＊　＊　＊

1960年代からはコラージュ作品が始まる。コラージュの素材は海外の雑誌や新聞、チラシ、使い古した布団や衣類、蚊帳など、どれも身の回りにあったもので、一般的にはゴミとして見過ごされるものも多い。《作品 63-5B》(1963年) では義母が長年使っていた藍染の生地を使い、《Work-64-I》(1964年、no. 9) では、三島茂司が持っていた海外の新聞や『LIFE』誌から切り取られたページが用いられている。この一連の作品の面白さは、コラージュという手法自体 (それ自体はキュビズムに始まったクラシックな手法) ではなく、そのモチーフが異種性であり、さらには、そのモチーフのほとんどが日常に根ざしているところなのではないだろうか。異種さは三島の好奇心の貪欲さを、そして日常は日々の生活の中に潜む「何か」を逃すことがない、三島の生まれ持った観察眼の鋭敏さを示している。

1960年代後半からは、そこにシルクスクリーン印刷が加わり、コラージュと油彩、アクリル絵具を用いた混合技法で、独自の平面表現を追求する。三島の平面作品は、この頃にひとつの完成形に到達したと考えられる。《ヴィーナスの変貌V》(1967年、no. 14) は、シルクスクリーンで刷られた3種類のヴィーナスが英字新聞を貼った支持体の上に印刷されている作品。さらに中央部には、穴が空いたような濃い色で塗りつぶされた矩形に、唯一色彩が反転されたヴィーナスが印刷されている。同時期の作品《作品68-A》(1968年、no. 15) にも、同じような矩形が描かれている。その背景には広告や雑誌のページなどもコラージュされていることが断片的に確認でき、オプ・アート[2]ようなストライプ・パターンが描かれている。前面には、そのほとんどを塗りつぶすような緑の矩形がベタ塗りされている。背景にある複数の絵画様式と、イメージを無効にするかのように存在する矩形は、新たに出現していた「虚無」を感じさせる。つまり、三島が描こうとしていたのは、現代における存在の孤独ではないか。三島は、凄まじいスピードで変貌を遂げようとする社会の中で、自己の存在の基底が揺らぐことへの恐怖を感じとったのかもしれない。《ヴィーナスの変貌V》でヴィーナスが立っていたのも、この虚無だったのだろうか。絶対的なヴィーナスですら、その存在やアイデンティティが揺らいでしまうとでもいうように。そして、この日常に潜む「恐怖」は、現在にいたるまで、三島の作品に通底するテーマになっていくのである。

油彩から始まり、コラージュ、そしてシルクスクリーンへ技法が変化する辺りから、三島の作品はポップ・アートと対比されることが増えてくる。美術評論家の建畠哲は、「コラージュ(印刷物の直接的な流用)から複製(シルクスクリーンによる転写)へという推移は、それが誰もが知るアイコンの導入でもあったことと相俟って、ネオダダからポップ・アートへの展開と見なすこともできなくはない」[3]と論じている。チラシや広告、アイコンの導入、またそれらのイメージの反復などにおいて、ポップ・アートの表現との近似性を確認できる。一方で、三島の作品がポップ・アートとは完全に一致していなかった点も指摘しておく必要がある。それが先述の「恐怖」である。

三島がコラージュやシルクスクリーンを用いた作品を制作していたのは、日本が高度経済成長期を迎えようとする時代で、社会に氾濫する情報が急速に増えていた状況に応答するものだった。三島は「どんな情報も読み終わった途端即全部ゴミになる」と考え、「現代社会に氾濫する膨大な情報に対する不安感や恐怖感」を覚えたという。チラシや雑誌などを用いたコラージュや印刷は、押し寄せる情報を作品に取り入れ、捨てられない形に定着させる方法だった。つまり、その根底には、資本主義・商業主義社会、それに伴う情報化社会への恐怖があったのである。その点において、大量生産など現代消費社会を礼賛するポップ・アートとは根本的に相容れないのである。[4]

「恐怖」を抱きながら、三島は陶の作品に進んでいく。三島は、ある時、飯茶碗が割れたのを見て、「ぱりんっ」と割れる新聞紙があったら「おもろい」と思った。陶で新聞を作るのに参考にしたのは、デパートの催事場で目にした、うどん作りの実演販売だという。うどんの生地を薄く伸ばす要領で土を薄く伸ばし、表面にはシルクスクリーンで印刷した陶器用の転写シートで施釉した。苦労の末、新聞紙は「ぱりんっ」と割れる性質を纏った。新聞やチラシという「情報」に、陶の質量を与えることで、情報が物質として重みを増し現実空間に作用する。また、割れてしまう脆さは、消費され無用になる儚さだけでなく、鋭利な破片となりうる危うさも暗示しているのかもしれない。三島が直感的に見抜いた「おもろさ」は、「恐怖」の対象であった情報の本質を物質化し、現実世界に引きずり出すことだったのである。

＊　＊　＊

1970年代以降から現在に至るまで、陶という素材は三島の制作において中心的なメディアとなっている。一方で、三島が陶というメディアに固執しているわけではないことにも留意すべきである。三島は、陶以外にもFRP（繊維強化プラスチック）やポリエステル繊維、スラグ等、多様な素材や技法を用いている。しかし、三島は長い間、陶芸作家として受容されてきたことも事実である。1971年の「第1回日本陶芸展 前衛部門」[5]（大丸百貨店［東京］、アメリカ、カナダ巡回）以降、毎年、国内外の陶芸や工芸のグループ展に参加している。受賞歴を見ても陶芸関係が圧倒的に多い。これはもちろん、三島が陶芸というメディアを用いていたことがその理由であるが、陶芸というメディアがもっている曖昧さや、1970年代以降にその定義が変化し続けていたことも大きいだろう。三島は「おもろい」ものを追求し続けていただけであったが、作品の受容を考察する上で重要な視点であるので、ここでメディアとしての陶芸の成り立ちを振り返りたい。

明治期以降、日本では陶芸の位置付けを巡る様々な議論がなされた。陶芸を含む工芸については「純粋美術」に対する「工業美術」、「純正美術」に対する「応用美術」という対比に始まり、「応用美術家」（工芸）は社会的なステータスにおいて「純正美術家」（美術）より劣るといった評価が生まれ、定着してしまった。三島がしばしば比較されることのある走泥社を始めとする前衛陶芸には、その固定概念からの逸脱という目的があった。例えば、オブジェ焼きといわれる走泥社の作品とは、「陶芸についての陶芸である。陶芸というメディアにとって本質的でない要素（例えば茶人趣味）をすべて削ぎ落とし、土、造形、釉薬、焼成といったプロセス自体を主題とする。陶芸の「素直」とは、陶芸メディアの純化＝あるがままの陶芸の再発見であり、陶芸批評／批判としての陶芸のことであった」[6]とされる。前衛陶芸が、陶芸のメディア批評であるモダニズムの表現であったことを考えると、三島の作品とは一線を画すものであることは明らかである。三島の興味はあくまでも、新聞や空き缶、段ボールなどが割れる「おもろさ」にあり、メディアとしての陶芸には無頓着で、走泥社に関しては「全然興味ない」[7]と断言している。

陶芸作家として認められた三島であったが、現代アートの文脈でも一定の評価を受けてきたことも事実である。そこには、1970年代後半から、現代アートの中で「もの派」や「アースワーク」など自然素材をメディアとする表現から派生した「クレイワーク」が生まれたことにより、1980年代に現代アートと陶芸において表現の相似化が進んだという背景もある。

1980年に国際芸術アカデミー総会が京都で開催され、協賛展として近代陶芸と抽象表現のオブジェなどを含む現代陶芸とを対照させた「クレイワーク—やきものから造形へ」展によってクレイワークが大きな流れになった。クレイワークは、結局のところ誰もしっかりと定義できない「中間性」、曖昧さを持ったまま、時代の表現となっていったという。三島も出展した2003年に国立国際美術館で開催された「大地の芸術 クレイワーク新世紀」のカタログには、「クレイワークという言葉は、日本で1970年前後ぐらいから陶芸関係者たちの間で造形的で前衛的なニュアンスを持つ言葉として、いくつかの留保条件をつけたりしながら、おっかなびっくりで使われはじめていたようである。(中略) クレイワークは、広範な意味として内容をもつ“セラミック”とは全然異なって、なんとなく実験的・前衛的陶芸、バタ臭い欧米風造形指向の陶芸などを意味するものとして理解されていたように見える」[8]と書かれている。こうした陶芸というメディアや、土という素材の曖昧さは、結果的に三島の作家性を捉えにくいものにしてしまった一因である。

しかし、先に述べた「ポップ・アート」「オプ・アート」「前衛・現代陶芸」「クレイワーク」など、三島の作品は様々な動向との近似性を仄めかすが、どれひとつとしてしっくりくるものはなかったことも事実である。それは、三島がひとりの美術作家として目覚めた戦後関西の前衛の時代に、どの団体にも属することなく、自分の興味に基づいて制作をしていた姿とも重なる。文脈や動向からの「距離感」などはお構いなく、「おもろさ」によって突き動かされ、その量も大きさも規格外の作品群を制作し続けていることがその証左である。同時に、その孤高な姿勢は、2023年に岐阜県現代陶芸美術館で開催された個展「三島喜美代ー遊ぶ 見つめる 創りだす」が、三島にとって初となる美術館での個展となってしまったという、遅すぎる評価を招いてしまった理由だといえるだろう。

近年、世界的にアートシーン自体が多様化され、アーティストを取り巻く環境は大きく変化している。近代以降の美術史が、植民地史観や欧米の白人男性アーティストを中心とする視点で記述されてきたことに対する反省から、非欧米圏のアーティストや女性アーティスト、LGBTQなど、周縁に追いやられていた出自のアーティスト達に注目が集まっている。こうした動向の中で、主流の文脈で語られてこなかった三島に改めて評価の目が向くことは自然な流れだろう。だからこそ、いま一度、三島の作品をこれまでの文脈とは異なる新たな視点から語り始めることが、必要とされているのではないだろうか。

＊　＊　＊

　では、どうして三島は新聞紙や広告、雑誌、ダンボール箱、空き缶など、同じモチーフを繰り返し用いるのか。いま一度、三島の表現におけるイメージやモチーフの連続性について考えてみたい。

　話は飛躍するが、文化人類学において研究対象として関心を向けられてきた「儀礼」に関する、レヴィ=ストロースの非常に鋭い考察がある。研究者の福島真人[9]によると、1970年代から80年代前半に象徴人類学や記号論が全盛の時、「儀礼へのアプローチとして影響力が強かったのは、そもそも儀礼の意味とは何か、あるいは儀礼に使われる様々な要素はどういう『象徴』なのか（つまり何を指しているのか）という問い」[10]であったという。その中でレヴィ＝ストロースは、「象徴解釈は、一種の『釈義』として、研究者や現地の人びとが断片的に作り出す神話のようなものであり、儀礼そのものではない」と批判し、儀礼の「核心は無限の反復行為であり、同じ行為を無限に繰り返すことで連続性を作り出す作業[11]」であるという革新的な主張をしたのである。確かに、伝統社会における儀礼をみると連続性という要素が散見される。身近なものには念仏などが挙げられるだろう。「レヴィ=ストロースはそうした無限の反復の中に『儀礼』の核を見出し、それを言説の体系である『神話』を鋭く対比させているのである」。[12]

　ここで若干強引ではあるが、三島の制作自体をひとつの儀礼として捉えてみると何が見えてくるだろう。三島は、同じモチーフを大量に、そして幾度も制作してきた。もちろん、新聞や雑誌の切り抜きの一部は、自身が興味のあるアーティストの記事など取捨選択されたものではあるが、重要なのはそうした個別の意味ではなく、メディアとしての全体である。モチーフを象徴的な意味から切り離し、その反復や、同じモチーフの作品を幾つも制作し続けてきたという行為の中の連続性に注目した時、それは「核」として何を意味するのだろうか。

　三島は、「人類の情報との関わりからくるあらゆる意味での矛盾の一側面を、陶芸化による異化作用を通じて顕在化させ、我々自身に情報の問題を再認識させる一つのきっかけでもあり続けてほしい」[13]と言う。三島にとって、同じものを大量に、そして幾度も制作することは、得体の知れない何かを捉えて認識する方法であり、また、恐怖の対象に近づこうとするアプローチなのである。

三島は自身の制作について「命がけで遊んでいる」[14]と言う。「おもろさ」に突き動かされ、命がけで制作に打ち込み続けるその姿は、現実という壁を前に祈りを捧げる儀礼のようにも見える。建畠は、大作《Work 92-N》(1990-92年、fig. 6) を「それは今日という時代に対峙する大いなるモニュメント」[15]と書いている。これを「祈りのモニュメント」とも言い換えることができるのではないだろうか。私達は、三島の祈りを通じて現実に対峙し、過去や未来について思いを馳せることができる。祈りであるからこそ、戦争や瓦礫、破滅に向かっている情報化社会の恐怖など、人類の負の遺産をまとっていたとしても人々の心に響き、あっけらかんとした「おもろさ」は、私たちを魅了し続けるのである。

(森美術館 アソシエイト・キュレーター)

註

1 ハンス・ウルリッヒ・オブリスト「三島喜美代は語る」『三島喜美代―Kimiyo Mishima』艸居、2021年、106頁
2 1960年代に起こった英国のアートムーブメント。その中心的なアーティストであるブリジット・ライリーの代表作である波形のストライプパターン(1967年ー)が、《作品68-A》(no. 15) のストライプと近似している偶然は興味深い。
3 建畠晢「大いなる逸脱の力学」『アナザー・エナジー展―挑戦しつづける力―世界の女性アーティスト16人』森美術館、257頁
4 三島とほぼ同世代の草間彌生が、1960年代にニューヨークでポップ・アートの作家として注目を集めていたが、「(機械で量産された) マカロニを一生食べて死ぬこともできないし、生きることもできない。ベルト・コンベアに乗せられたみたいで、パニック状態になるって私は思った」※と語っており、消費社会に対して同様の恐怖を抱いていたこと、そして、それが曲解されポップ・アートとして受容されたという偶然は非常に興味深い。
※ 三浦清宏、草間彌生「対談」『草間彌生 ニューヨーク/東京』淡交社、1999年、22頁
※ "In Full Bloom: Yayoi Kusama, Years in Japan, " Tankosha, 1999, p.22
5 The 1st Japan Ceramic Art exhibition, Avant-garde section, Daimaru Department Store, Tokyo, Japan; touring in U.S.A. and Canada
6 清水穣「陶芸の「勢い」について　鯉江良二論」『陶芸考　現代日本の陶芸家たち』2016年、24頁
7 ハンス・ウルリッヒ・オブリスト「三島喜美代は語る」『三島喜美代―Kimiyo Mishima』艸居、2021年、115頁
8 安來正博「クレイワークの座標―80年代から現在までの状況」『大地の芸術―クレイワーク新世紀』国立国際美術館、2003年、109頁
9 科学・技術への人類学的アプローチ (STS: Social studies of science and technology)、現代的制度 (実験室、病院、組織) の社会人類学、認知と学習の理論、比較宗教学など幅広い研究を行う。
10 福島真人「「象徴の森」の内と外―テクノサイエンス時代の『儀礼の過程』」ヴィクター・W.ターナー『儀礼の過程』(冨倉光雄訳) 筑摩書房、2020年、359頁
11 福島、361頁
12 同上
13 建畠、257頁
14 同上
15 同上

Analysis of "Fun" in the Art of Mishima Kimiyo

Tokuyama Hirokazu

The charm of Mishima Kimiyo's work lies in its unaffected, spirited vitality. Her dynamic works exude energy like a clear blue sky piercing through the clouds, refreshing the viewer with each encounter. At the same time, they are consistently underpinned by a critical gaze towards contemporary society. Mishima's works cast doubt on aspects of everyday life that we usually take for granted, laying bare the inherent fragility lurking beneath. However, they contain no trace of the dogmatic or doctrinaire. They simply shed brilliant light on the realities of our world, with all their contradictions.

When asked about her motivation for making something, Mishima responds in Kansai (a region of western Japan) dialect, "I just thought it would be fun." With regard to particular motifs or techniques, she states in no uncertain terms, "It simply seemed like a fun idea. I didn't think deeply about it." Whether it's a newspaper, a trash bin full of empty beverage cans, or a Sunkist cardboard box, she comments that replicating it with ceramics seemed like a fun idea. Her motivations are pure and truly unpretentious. This essay will explore the sense of fun that drives Mishima and how it has been perceived in the context of art, and building on this foundation, will re-examine implications of Mishima's art that only become clear through the lens of her entire, 70-year-plus career arc.

Mishima Kimiyo was born in Juso, Osaka to parents who ran a coffee shop. She took an interest in painting while attending a girls' high school (the equivalent of a present-day junior high school), where her homeroom teacher was a painter, prompting her to start painting in oils. World War II ended during her first year at the school, bringing about changes including a shift in art education's focus away from copying after designated pictures, allowing for a freer approach to painting. At the time, Mishima did not yet aspire to be a painter or any kind of artist, but hoped to go to medical school and become a researcher. She had owned five microscopes since early childhood, and enjoyed scrutinizing various things under them, including insects and her own hair.[1] She has said that her greatest goal as a researcher was to clone a human being. When she mentioned this to her mother, her mother consulted a medical doctor she knew, who admonished her that "creating a human being would be a blasphemy against God." This led Mishima to abandon her dream of pursuing medical studies. After graduating from the girls' high school, she immersed herself in oil painting and met her future husband, Mishima Shigeji (1920-1985), in the painting class he taught. She also encountered the avant-garde through Shigeji, who had studied with Yoshihara Jiro (1905-1972), leader of the Gutai Art Association. This further propelled her toward pursuing a career in art.

Mishima graduated from school around 1947. Given that it was not until 1997 that Dolly the cloned sheep was born, Mishima's curiosity, imagination, and prescience regarding human cloning fifty years earlier are extraordinary. The Kansai region in the 1950s, when Mishima began painting seriously, was fertile ground for the emergence of new modes of expression. After World War II, Japan raced to reconstruct the nation and rebound as quickly as possible from the poverty caused by the war, leading to radical changes in people's value systems and the political and economic landscape. Similarly, the art world was undergoing a major transition. In the postwar years, the Kansai region alone was home to over 60 artist associations, and young artists sought modes of art that resonated with the era's new ideologies, giving rise to various movements.

Mishima initially began making art out of a pure desire to paint, but over time she seems to have made painting a more personal form of expression, as reflected in her shift from figuration to abstraction. Influenced by the Art Informel movement that originated in Europe and was sweeping Japan, Mishima prolifically produced abstract paintings. From 1954 to 1969, she exhibited with Dokuritsu Bijutsu Kyokai (the Independent Art Association), winning the Dokuritsu Prize in 1963 and an honorable mention at the Shell Art Award exhibition in 1965, steadily advancing her career. While Mishima did not belong to any specific group, the general fervor for novel expression in the postwar Kansai region appears to have fed her exploration of a unique artistic language, or in her words a "fun" mode of expression. This exploration mirrors her childhood obsession with looking through microscopes.

In the 1960s, she began working with collage. The materials for her collages included foreign magazines, newspapers, flyers, used futons, clothing, and mosquito nets, all of which she found in her surroundings, and much of which would typically be dismissed as trash. In *Work 63-5B* (1963) she incorporated indigo-dyed fabric that her mother-in-law had been using for many years, and in *Work-64-I* (1964, no. 9) there are pages cut from foreign newspapers and issues of *Life* magazine belonging to her husband. This series of works is fascinating not merely for its use of collage, a classic technique going back to Cubism, but for the heterogeneity of its motifs and the fact that most were firmly rooted in everyday life. The heterogeneity reflects Mishima's voracious curiosity, while the focus on the mundane highlights her innately keen observational skills, directed toward a hidden "something" lurking beneath the surface of day-to-day routines.

In the late 1960s, Mishima began incorporating silkscreen printing into her mixed-media works along with collage, oil, and acrylic, developing a unique style in her two-dimensional works. It can be said that her work on flat surfaces reached a culmination of sorts during this period. *Transfiguration of Venus V* (1967, no. 14) features three different images of the goddess silkscreened onto a support covered with English newspapers. In the center, a dark painted rectangle evoking a hole contains another image of Venus, which unlike the rest of the picture has its colors reversed. A similar rectangle appears in *Work 68-A* (1968, no. 15), which features a background of collaged fragments of ads and magazine pages and a striped pattern reminiscent of Op Art.[2] In the foreground, these elements are almost completely obscured by a solidly painted green rectangle. The multiple painting styles in the background, and the rectangle that seems to negate the images, suggest an emerging awareness of "the void." Perhaps what Mishima sought to convey was the isolation of life in the contemporary world. Amid a drastically changing society, Mishima seems to have experienced dread toward the unstable foundations of her own existence. Does the goddess in *Transfiguration of Venus*

V stand in this void, as if the existence and identity of even an absolute divinity like Venus is in flux? This "dread" lurking beneath the surface of the everyday became a recurring theme in Mishima's art, and remains so to this day.

Mishima started out with oils, began incorporating collage and then silkscreen, and her works increasingly came to be compared with Pop Art. The art critic Tatehata Akira noted, "Her transition from collage (direct appropriation of printed materials) to reproduction (transfer via silkscreen) suggests a progression from Neo-Dada to Pop, particularly with the introduction of universally recognizable icons."[3] The introduction of flyers, advertisements, and icons, as well as the repetition of images, confirms their proximity to Pop. However, it must be noted that Mishima's works did not completely align with Pop Art, and this relates to the aforementioned sense of dread.

Mishima's use of collage and silkscreen was a response to Japan's rapid economic growth period, during which there was a drastic increase in the volume of information flooding society. In Mishima's view, "all information instantly becomes trash as soon as it is consumed," and says that she felt "a sense of anxiety and dread toward the massive glut of information in present-day society." Her collage and printing practice, employing flyers or magazines, was a way of incorporating this tsunami of information into her works, fixing it in place so it could not be discarded. In essence, underlying this approach was fear of capitalism, commercialism, and the information society that accompanied it. In this regard, her work fundamentally contradicted Pop, which generally celebrated mass production and contemporary consumer society.[4]

Still harboring this dread, Mishima shifted toward ceramics. One day, on seeing a rice bowl break, she thought it would be entertaining to see a newspaper break with the same crisp, cracking sound. In crafting ceramic newspapers, she took cues from a live udon noodle-making demonstration that she saw at a department store. With the same process used to roll out thin sheets of dough for noodles, she made thin sheets of clay and glazed them using silkscreen-printed ceramic transfer sheets. After much effort, she succeeded in producing newspapers that would break crisply. By endowing information, in the form of newspapers and flyers, with the physical mass of ceramics, she gave the information material weight and presence in the real world. The works' fragility took on an additional dimension, as it not only signified the transience of quickly being consumed and rendered useless, but also hinted at the danger they posed if shattered into sharp fragments. The "fun" that Mishima intuitively sensed could be had involved rendering the essence of the information, which had been an object of dread, in material form, and forcing it into the real world.

Ceramics have central to Mishima's practice from the 1970s until the present day. However, it should be noted that Mishima is not exclusively committed to this medium, but also employs a variety of other materials and techniques, including FRP (fiber-reinforced plastic), polyester textiles, and slag. Nonetheless, Mishima has long been recognized predominantly as a ceramic artist. Since her participation in the Avant-Garde Section of the 1st Japan Ceramic Exhibition (1971)[5] at the Daimaru Department Store in Tokyo, which later toured the US and Canada, every year she has taken part in ceramic and craft group exhibitions both in Japan and abroad. Her awards, too, have been almost entirely in the ceramics field. This of course reflects her frequent use of the medium, but it is also important to note the ambiguity of ceramics as a medium and the fact that its definition has continued to change since the 1970s. While Mishima has continued to pursue what strikes her as "fun," understanding the evolution of ceramics as a medium is crucial for interpretation of the reception of Mishima's work, so let us review it here.

Since the Meiji era (1868-1912), there has been abundant and varied discourse on ceramics in Japan. Debates on crafts, including ceramics, initially placed "industrial arts" in opposition to "pure arts," or "applied arts" in contrast to "fine arts," eventually establishing a social hierarchy in which applied artists (or crafts) were deemed inferior in status to fine artists (or fine art). Avant-garde ceramics groups such as Sodeisha, to which Mishima's work is frequently compared, challenged these conventional views. Sodeisha members' works, termed *objet-yaki* (ceramic objects), were "ceramics as ceramics," focusing on the core elements of the medium – clay, forms, glazing, firing – and stripping away any non-essential elements such as tea ceremony aesthetics. This was viewed as "a rediscovery of 'plain' or 'honest' ceramics, and as both a critique of and a critical engagement with the medium."[6] If avant-garde ceramics were a modernist endeavor, self-referentially critiquing their own medium, then they stand in stark contrast to Mishima's works. Her primary concern has been with the fun derived from rendering breakable such everyday objects as newspapers, cans, and cardboard boxes. She lacks concern with ceramics as a medium per se, and has stated her total lack of interest in Sodeisha.[7]

Mishima has been perceived as a ceramic artist, but she has also achieved a certain degree of recognition in the context of contemporary art. In the late 1970s, the genre known as "clay work" emerged in the lineage of other movements employing natural materials such as Mono-ha (the "School of Things") and earthworks (also known as land art). This led to a convergence of contemporary art and ceramics in the 1980s.

In 1980, the International Art and Culture Academy held a general assembly in Kyoto, and in conjunction, the exhibition *Clay Work: From Traditional to Avant-Garde* showcased contemporary ceramics, juxtaposing modern ceramics, abstract objects and so forth and establishing clay work as a recognized genre in Japan. Ultimately, clay work was hobbled by "intermediacy" and ambiguity that defied definitive categorization, and did not endure, but rather became representative of that art-historical moment. In the catalogue for *The Art of Earth: Clay Works of the New Century* at the National Museum of Art, Osaka in 2003, in which Mishima participated, it is noted: "The term 'clay work,' with sculptural and avant-garde nuances, began to be used by ceramicists in Japan around the early 1970s, albeit timidly and with some reservations... It appears that clay work was perceived as completely different from 'ceramics' broadly defined, applying to experimental and avant-garde ceramics, or ceramics with a somewhat derivative Western-style formal orientation."[8] This ambiguity regarding ceramics as a medium and clay as a material is part of what has made it challenging to fully grasp Mishima's artistic identity.

However, as previously mentioned, while Mishima's works suggest proximity to various movements such as Pop Art, Op Art, avant-garde and contemporary ceramics, and clay work, it is also the case that none of these fit perfectly. This is in line with the fact that Mishima, emerging as an individual artist during the flourishing of the avant-garde in postwar Kansai, belonged to no group and made things based on her own interests. This is evidenced by the way in which she had no concern with "distance" from contexts or movements, was motivated by "fun," and has continued prolifically producing works that are unconventional in terms of both volume and size. This solitary stance has also unfortunately resulted in belated recognition, with her first solo show at a museum not occurring until 2023 when *Mishima Kimiyo: Play Watch Create* was held at the Museum of Modern Ceramic Art, Gifu.

In recent years, the global art scene has diversified, and the environment surrounding artists has greatly changed. Modern art history, which has been narrated from colonialist perspectives and centered on white, male, Western artists, is now undergoing a course correction, focusing attention on previously marginalized artists including those from from non-Western regions, women, and LGBTQ individuals. In this climate, it is only natural for new light to be shed on Mishima, who had been outside the mainstream narrative. For this reason, it seems necessary to discuss Mishima's works from new perspectives that depart from previous contexts.

So, why does Mishima consistently deal with the same subjects, such as newspapers, ads, magazines, cardboard boxes, and empty cans? Here, let us address the continuity of images and motifs in Mishima's art.

First, to digress for a moment, Claude Lévi-Strauss had extremely keen insights regarding rituals, a major focus of cultural anthropology. According to the researcher Fukushima Masato,[9] during the heyday of symbolic anthropology and semiotics in the 1970s and early 1980s, "the dominant approach focused on the fundamental meanings of rituals and what their various elements 'symbolized' or meant."[10] In this context, Lévi-Strauss critically noted that "symbolic interpretation, as a form of 'exegesis,' is like a myth cobbled together by researchers or devised by the people being studied, and is not intrinsic to the ritual itself," and proposed the groundbreaking notion that "the essence of a ritual lies in its infinite repetition, which creates continuity through endless reiteration of the same actions."[11] Indeed, such continuity is a consistent feature of the rituals of traditional societies. An example familiar to Japanese observers is the chanting of *nenbutsu* (prayers to Buddha). "Lévi-Strauss pointed to indefinite repetition as lying at the core of rituals, and sharply contrasted this with the discursive frameworks of mythology."[12]

At the risk of overstating my case, I believe that viewing Mishima's creative process in terms of ritual may deliver new insights. Mishima has consistently produced works with the same motifs over many years, and in vast numbers. While some of the newspapers and magazine clippings are deliberately selected, including articles on artists who interest her, the core of her practice lies not in these individual meanings but in the overall media context. When we turn our attention to continuity in the repeated and sustained creation of multiple works with the same subject matter, what does this "core of her practice" signify?

Mishima has said, "Through the process of transforming everyday objects into ceramics, I aim to expose one aspect of the contradictions inherent in humanity's relationship to information, and to continually offer opportunities for us to reassess problems and issues surrounding information."[13] For her, repeatedly making the same objects in large quantities is a means of capturing and perceiving things that would otherwise remain elusive, and a way of confronting the objects of her dread.

Mishima has described her own creative process as "playing as if my life were at stake."[14] Driven by the pursuit of "fun," and dedicating herself wholeheartedly to her art, she resembles someone ritualistically offering prayers before the wall that is reality. Tatehata wrote of the large-scale *Work 92-N* (1990-92, fig. 6), "It is a powerful monument that confronts the current era."[15] It could also be described as a "monument of prayer." Through Mishima's prayer-like practice, viewers are able to engage with reality and reflect on the past and the future. And because of this prayer-like quality, her unabashed spirit of fun continues to captivate us even when the works reflect humanity's dark legacy of wars, rubble, and the dread pervading an information-saturated society that appears headed for extinction.

Associate Curator, Mori Art Museum

Notes

1. Hans Ulrich Obrist, "Mishima Kimiyo Speaks," *Mishima Kimiyo*, Sokyo, 2021, p. 106.
2. Op Art was a movement that emerged in the UK in the 1960s. It is an intriguing coincidence that the trademark wavy striped patterns (from 1967 onward) of Bridget Riley, an artist at the forefront of this movement, resemble the stripes in Mishima's *Work 68-A*.
3. Tatehata Akira, "*Oi naru itsudatsu no rikigaku*" [Dynamics of Great Deviation], Another Energy, Mori Art Museum, p. 257.
4. Kusama Yayoi, of roughly of the same generation as Mishima, gained renown as a Pop artist in New York in the 1960s. However, she has said, "I could not live on macaroni [mass-produced by machine] for the rest of my life. It makes me feel like I am on a conveyor belt, in a state of panic."* It is a deeply intriguing coincidence that Kusama harbored a similar dread towards consumer society, and that her sentiments were also misunderstood and interpreted as being in the spirit of Pop Art.

* Miura Kiyohiro, Kusama Yayoi, "Taidan" [Dialogue], *Kusama Yayoi: New York / Tokyo*, Tankosha, 1999, p. 22.

*"In Full Bloom: Yayoi Kusama, Years in Japan," Tankosha, 1999, p. 22.

5. The 1st Japan Ceramic Art exhibition, Avant-Garde Section, Daimaru Department Store, Tokyo, Japan; touring the US and Canada.
6. Shimizu Minoru, "Togei no 'ikioi' ni tsuite: Koie Ryoji ron" [On the 'Force' of Ceramics: Koie Ryoji], *Togeiko: Gendai Nihon no togeisha tachi* [Ceramic Thought: Contemporary Japanese Ceramicists], 2016, p. 24.
7. Hans Ulrich Obrist, "Mishima Kimiyo Speaks," *Mishima Kimiyo*, Sokyo, 2021, p. 115.
8. Yasugi Masahiro, "The Position of Clay Work: History from the '80s to Today," *The Art of Earth: Clay Works of the New Century*, The National Museum of Art, Osaka, 2003, p. 109.
9. Fukushima's research covers a wide range of topics, including STS (Science and Technology Studies, i.e. an anthropological approach to science and technology), the social anthropology of contemporary institutions (laboratories, hospitals, organizations), theories of cognition and learning, and comparative religion.
10. Fukushima Masato, " '*Shocho no mori' no uchi to soto: techno science jidai no* Girei no katei" [Inside and Outside the "Forest of Symbols": The Ritual Process in a Techno-Scientific Era], *The Ritual Process*, Chikumashobo, 2020, p. 359.
11. Fukushima, p. 361.
12. Ibid.
13. Tatehata, p. 257.
14. Ibid.
15. Ibid.

パキッとしていて、ぐちゃぐちゃなもの

森村泰昌

光工業のこと

JR大阪環状線の鶴橋駅を降りて約5分のところに、光工業があった。2年くらい前、突然解体工事がはじまり、コインパーキングになった。27台分の駐車スペースに加え、電動キックボードのシェアリングサービスも完備している。

それなりに大きいこの駐車場から目と鼻の先に私の仕事場がある。生まれ育ったのも、いま暮らしているのも、そこからすぐそこのところである。

だから三島喜美代さんが「鶴橋のなんちゃらいうところ、よう行ってました。せやからいっつもモリムラさんの仕事場の前、通ってました」と、頬にエクボを作って楽しそうにお話になったときは、やっぱりうれしかった。「なんちゃらいうところ」が光工業だと、すぐにわかったからである。

でも、ずっと近くに住んでいるのに、うかつにも、光工業さんがどういう会社なのかよく知らなかった。通りすがりにチラチラ見ているかぎりでは、店舗向けの飾り物を造るディスプレイ会社のように思えたが、守備範囲はもっとひろそうだった。

三島さんはいったいここで何を発注していたのだろう。シルクスクリーンの版なのか、立体制作のための成型品なのか。三島さんにそのことは聞きそびれたままになっている。

ジョルジュ・ブラックに始まる

《マスカット》(no. 1)という三島さんの初期油絵がある。制作年は1951年。この年に私は、あの光工業さんの近くで生まれたわけだ。

《マスカット》を見ていると、高校生時代を思いだす。美術クラブに入部して油絵に夢中になっていたあの頃、私はジョルジュ・ブラックが好きだった。品のいいキュビズム。そんな感じで好きだった。しかしブラックみたいな絵を描こうとしてもうまくいかず、おおいに悩んでいた。

それなのに三島さんはどうだ。ちゃんとブラックを自分のものにしたステキな絵を、私が生まれた年にすでに描いている。

三島さんがブラックを意識していたかどうかはわからない。でも、あの《マスカット》と、1951年と、ジョルジュ・ブラックを強引につなげると、かつて若者の私が生きていた1960年代がふつふつと蘇ってくる。

ブラックのあと私は抽象画に走った。日本の抽象画が好きで、菅井汲さんに憧れた。アンフォルメル調のマチエールがきわ立つ初期作品も、その後の色と形がパキッと張りつめた感じの幾何学的抽象画も好きだった。

私もあんな絵を描きたいとがんばった。そんな10代の頃の思い出があるので、

三島さんから菅井汲さんとの出会いのことを聞いたときは驚いた。

三島さんの1960年代後半の絵には、アンフォルメルを抜けだして、アンディ・ウォーホルやラウシェンバーグを取りこもうという強い意志が感じられるが、同時に菅井汲がそこにいる。

と、かってに思いこんでいるのだが、それはともかく、菅井さんの作品、ステキですよねえと、やっぱり私は三島さんとおおいに語りあいたいのである。

パキッ!、が好き

菅井汲さんの絵はパキッとしている。ポルシェに乗っておられたと聞く。パキッとしたカッコいい絵と、ポルシェで高速道路を疾駆する男前の菅井さんが重なって見えてくる。

三島さんが絵を離れて、「陶」という素材を選択されたのも、あのパキッとした感覚をさらに高めていくためのジャンプ、決意表明だったのではないだろうか。

三島さんの「陶」には、土の塊という重々しい感じがない。なにせ新聞や空き缶がモチーフで、私はいつも煎餅を想起してしまう。煎餅を食べるときのあのパリ感が、三島さんの「陶」にはいつもある。

薄い「陶」でできた新聞紙は割れると、まるで煎餅のようにパキッと音がする(ような気がする)。それは絵画における鮮やかな色彩や色面のパキッとしたイメージが、「陶」という物質へと置きかえらえた、その感触の音なのである。

私の好きな三島作品に、産業廃棄物を粉末にした溶融スラグの作品がある。一見重厚に感じるのだが、さほど重くはないらしい。土状の塊に見えて、実際はがらんどうだからである。それで私には作品がふっくらとした巨大な揚げ餅みたいに見えてくる。

揚げ物と餅がともに好物である私には、この「パリッ、パキッ」のサクサク感がたまらない。

ぐちゃぐちゃにする

ところが三島さんには、「パキッ!」とは対照的なもうひとつのこだわりがある。それが「ぐちゃぐちゃ」、である。

あるビデオインタヴューで、新作について三島さんはこんなふうに語っておられる。少し長いが文字起こししてみた。*

もっとね　なんかぐちゃぐちゃにちらかしたかった　けっこうね　わーっとやりたかったんですけど　さわっているうちに　なんかおさまってしまって　きれいになってしもていうかんじはありますね　なんかさくひんかしてしまって　もうちょっとこれなんだあっていうように　ぐちゃぐちゃにしたかったんですけどね　それがああでもないこうでないて　さわっているうちに　やっぱりいつものくせがでてか　さくひんになってしまって　それだけがちょっとざんねんかなあっていうかんじはあるんですけど　うーん　ごらんになるかたにしたら　このほうがいいいうひとおおいですよ　そらそうですね　おちついてみれますから　ぐちゃぐちゃにして　なんやこれっていうてもらおかなあいうかんじやったんですけど　ぐちゃぐちゃにするのがむずしい　ぎゃくにいうたら

三島さんの本来の持ち味はパキッとした表現力にある。パキッと決める高い造形能力の持ち主で、それはあの1951年の《マスカット》にすでに現れていた。

それなのにと言うべきか、それゆえにと言うべきか、三島さんは自分自身の造形センスが、むしろ余計な打算に感じられ、人間の入れ知恵を働かせる余地のない「ぐちゃぐちゃ」を目指そうとする。誤解を恐れずに例えるなら、それは精魂込めて制作した「陶」の新聞紙を自らの手でパキパキッと破壊するのにも等しい荒事である。

パキッと張りつめた美意識は、あの高速道路を突っ走るポルシェが、事故を起こせば、一瞬にしてぐちゃぐちゃになるのと同様の危険を持っている。ほんとうの「パキッ!」は、「ぐちゃぐちゃ」と紙一重なのである。「ぐちゃぐちゃ」への覚悟がないようでは、いつまでたっても「パキッ!」となんかしてこない。

蛇足ながら、三島喜美代の作品は、「パキッ!」であれ、「ぐちゃぐちゃ」であれ、いつも不思議なくらい物静かである。ぶっつぶしてやるぞと息巻くような、下品な怒号からはほど遠く、静謐の気配が漂っている。

新聞紙も、空き缶も、産業廃棄物も、みんなゴミと見なされ、沈黙のうちに耐えている。三島さんは、その沈黙を本気で愛している。愛してみんなでいっしょに立ちあがろうよと、後押ししつづけている。その後押しが作品となる。

沈黙にまさる饒舌はない。
三島作品がその証であると私は思う。

（美術家）

＊「ごみと美術のあいだ2　三島喜美代インタビュー」聞き手・石田克哉（MEM）、2020年より
文字起こししたのは、三島さんが《Work20-G》（2017-2020）について語っている箇所である。

Making Things Snap, and Making a Mess

Morimura Yasumasa

Hikari Kogyo

About a five-minute walk from Tsuruhashi Station on the JR Osaka Loop Line, there used to be a company called Hikari Kogyo. About two years ago, they suddenly started demolishing the building, and the site is now a coin-operated parking lot. The lot can accommodate 27 vehicles, and even offers an e-scooter sharing service.

My studio is just steps away from this parking lot. I was born and raised very close by, and live right nearby today.

So, when Mishima Kimiyo reminisced with a dimpled smile, "I often visited what's-it-called, this place in Tsuruhashi, and I would walk right by Morimura-san's studio," I was quite charmed. I immediately understood that the "what's-it-called" she spoke of was Hikari Kogyo.

But despite living right around the corner, I must admit I didn't know much about what kind of company Hikari Kogyo was. From glancing at it as I walked by, I got the sense that they specialized in decorative store displays, but they seemed to offer a lot of other services as well.

What could Mishima-san have been ordering from them? Were they silkscreens, or molded objects for sculptures? Unfortunately, I've never had the chance to ask her more about that.

Beginning with Braque

There's an early oil painting by Mishima titled *Muscats* (no. 1), dated 1951. That's the year I was born near the aforementioned Hikari Kogyo.

Looking at *Muscats* brings me back to my high school years, when I belonged to the school art club and devoted myself to oil painting.

In those days I was particularly drawn to the elegant Cubist works of Georges Braque. However, when I tried to paint like Braque it did not go well, and I ended up quite frustrated.

Meanwhile, by the year I was born, Mishima-san was already making wonderful paintings that captured the essence of Braque's style, but were all her own.

I don't know whether Mishima was directly influenced by Braque. However, when I make the (admittedly tenuous) connections between *Muscats*, the year 1951, and Georges Braque, it stirs vivid memories of my youth in the 1960s.

After my Braque phase, I threw myself into abstraction. I was fond of Japanese abstract painting, and admired Sugai Kumi. I was drawn to both his early works, with rich materiality in the style of Art Informel, and his later geometric abstract paintings with a vivid palette and hard-edged forms.

In my teenage years, I did my best to paint such paintings myself. That made me all the more surprised to that Mishima-san had been closely acquainted with Sugai Kumi.

Mishima-san's works from the late 1960s show a strong ambition to transcend Art Informel, integrating influences from Andy Warhol and Rauschenberg, while Sugai is still there in the mix as well.

That's just my own interpretation. In any case, my admiration for Sugai remains undimmed, and I would love to talk with Mishima-san about this thing we share in common.

Snap!

Sugai Kumi's paintings snap, which is to say they're hard and crisp. I've heard he drove a Porsche, and his sharp, stylish paintings merge in my mind with the image of Sugai himself, a dashing figure in his Porsche speeding down the freeway.

Mishima-san's shift from painting to clay as a medium could well be seen as an endeavor to intensify that kind of crisp impression, a signal of her resolve to *snap*.

Mishima-san's ceramic works don't feel heavy like masses of clay. When she depicts motifs like newspapers and empty beverage cans, I am always reminded of rice crackers. For me, the *crunchy* sensation of eating a rice cracker is always present in her ceramic works.

When thin, fragile ceramic newspapers break (I imagine), they make a snapping sound like a rice cracker. It's as if the vibrant palette and color planes of her paintings have been transferred to the material domain of ceramics, and their textures translate to sound in my mind.

Among my favorite of Mishima-san's works are the ones made with molten slag, made from powdered industrial waste. Despite their hefty, imposing look, I hear they are surprisingly light. They resemble solid masses of earth but are essentially hollow, making me think of gigantic, fluffy fried rice crackers.

For someone like me with a penchant for fried foods and rice crackers, the crispy, crunchy *snap* of Mishima-san's works is irresistible.

Making a Mess

In contrast with the sharp *snap!* of her aesthetic, Mishima-san also harbors a fascination with messiness.

In a video interview, Mishima-san speaks about one of her new works. I've transcribed it here, at some length:*

"I wanted to scatter things more messily, really go wild with it. But as things turned out, somehow they settled down into neat-looking forms. Like, I sort of finished the work and wished I could've made it messier, so it would be like 'what the heck is this?' But as I worked on it, my usual habits came out, or it just turned into 'a work of art' on its own. That's kind of too bad, from my perspective. But, as for viewers, most of them prefer it this way. That makes sense, it's more relaxing to look at. I had wanted to make a mess and have people wonder, 'What on earth is that?' But you'd be surprised at how difficult it is to make things messy, actually."

Mishima-san's crispness of expression, her *snap*, is her secret weapon. She has extraordinary formal ability to make things fit into place. This is already evident in a work as old as her 1951 painting *Muscats*.

Mishima seemingly pursues "messiness," a state devoid of excessive calculation and human contrivance, in spite of – or should I say because of – her keen command of form, which she may feel is overly precise. If I may be so bold as to make this comparison, her practice is like the act of meticulously crafting a ceramic newspaper only to intentionally shatter it.

Her sharp aesthetic is imbued with a sense of peril, like the thrill of a Porsche racing along the freeway, where one false move would result in a catastrophic accident. There's a fine line separating the clean *snap* from a chaotic mess. There is no true *snap* without the willingness to confront mess and disorder.

Whether they come down on the side of *snap!* or the mess, Mishima Kimiyo's works always radiate remarkable tranquility. They are very far removed from threatening, wanton rage. They whisper rather than shouting.

Newspapers, empty cans, industrial waste—all are dismissed as unwanted garbage, a role they endure in silence. Mishima-san's genuine affection for this silence drives her to lead a rebellion of the discarded, which takes the form of her works.

There is nothing more eloquent than silence. I believe Mishima-san's art stands as a testament to this.

Artist

* From "*Gomi to bijutsu no aida 2* [Between Garbage and Art 2]: Mishima Kimiyo interview," interviewer: Ishida Katsuya (MEM), 2020.

In the transcribed passage, Mishima-san discusses her *Work 20-G* (2017-2020).

未来への記憶―三島喜美代展に寄せて

伊東正伸

近年、国内外からの評価がとみに高まっている現代美術家・三島喜美代さんのこれまでの仕事を振り返る展覧会を、当館において開催できますことを心から嬉しく思います。三島さんにとっては、これが東京の美術館における最初の個展となることから、近作展とはせずにあえて回顧展的な構成とし、初期の絵画作品から陶による立体作品シリーズ「割れる印刷物」、大型インスタレーション《20世紀の記憶》（1984–2013年、no. 82）、そして近作に至るまでの展開を辿ることとしました。展覧会を通して、三島さんが社会の現実を見つめながら、情報とゴミの問題をテーマに70年にわたって一貫して追い求めてきた作品世界を紹介いたします。

私が三島さんと初めてお会いしたのは、2017年1月のことです。国際交流基金の海外巡回展「超絶技巧の日本」の開催にともない、三島さんの陶による空き缶作品の出品をお願いするため、東京大田区のART FACTORY城南島を訪ねました。お目当ての空き缶作品は、屑籠の中に放り込まれたかのような体裁で、一つ一つのピースが精巧を極め、「超絶技巧」と呼ぶにふさわしいものでした。陶の表面にはシルクスクリーンで文字を転写印刷し、手彩色を施したポップでカラフルな仕上げによって陶の素材感は完全に消し去られています。鑑賞者は「缶」が陶でできていることを危うく見過ごしそうになりながらも、よりよく観察して事実に気づくと、驚きとともについ笑みがこぼれてしまうのです。私はその場で空き缶作品の出品を三島さんに依頼し、快諾をいただいたのでした。

しかし何といっても当日もっとも衝撃的だったのは、本展でもご覧いただく三島さん最大規模のインスタレーション作品《20世紀の記憶》でした。圧倒的なスケールによるこの作品は20×10メートルを超える空間に立ち現われ、高い密集度がもたらす張り詰めた空気が会場を支配します。まるで時間が凍結してしまったかのような沈黙の世界を目の当たりにして、私はしばし呆然と立ち尽くす以外にありませんでした。先ほどまでお話ししていた華奢な三島さんからは想像もつかない桁外れなインスタレーションで、しかも途方もなく根を詰めた作品でもあるのです。

《20世紀の記憶》は、床一面に耐火レンガ・ブロック約10,600個を敷き詰め、その表面には、三島さんが20世紀の100年間から抜き出した新聞記事等がシルクスクリーンの技法を用いて刷り込まれています。紙媒体の情報を陶へと転写しオブジェ化する、そうした制作行為を三島さんは「情報の化石化」と呼びますが、この作品は文字通り20世紀の膨大な情報を宿しているとともに、その時代に向き合った彼女自身の記憶も刻まれているのではないかと私は想像します。各レンガの表面には日本語の新聞記事、裏面には外国語の新聞記事が転写され、「日英攻守同盟」「人類　今日月に立つ」「利根川教授にノーベル賞」「0157」など特定のテーマに限定されない雑多な記事や見出しが躍ります。しかし、そのなかでも戦時色の濃い文言が否応なく目立つのは、20世紀という時代が戦争に明け暮れていたことを図らずも示していると言えるでしょう。レンガは、かつて土岐市の窯で台として使用されていた古レンガを再利用しているため、一部が欠けていたり、変色しているものも数多くあり、この不揃いさが空間全体に不穏さをもたらしています。1万個のレンガが織りなす景色は、情報過多の社会の行き着く先を露わにしたSF風の終末世界のようであり、はたまた戦争によって焼け野原になってしまった都市の廃墟をそこに見る人もいるでしょう。作品は黙して語らず、尋常ならざる気配だけが漂います。

私は期せずして、ヴェネチア・ビエンナーレ1993のドイツ館で見たハンス・ハーケ氏のインスタレーション《ゲルマニア》[1]を思い浮かべました。同作品は、1934年にドイツ館を視察したヒトラーの写真を正面入口に掲げ、ヒトラーの時代に再建された建物の大理石の床を破壊して鑑賞者にその上を歩かせるもので、この場所でなくては意味をなさない作品として成立していました。その点から言えば、場所性に固執せず、既存空間を変容させる《20世紀の記憶》とは明らかに異なっています。さらに《ゲルマニア》が制作に手数をかけず、最短ルートで核心を衝いているのに対し、《20世紀の記憶》はレンガ・ブロックを過剰なまでに集積させて物量感で圧しており、むしろ両作品は対照的と言っていいのかもしれません。しかしながら、ほぼ同時期に制作された作品として、ともに廃墟のような光景を現出させ、歴史の断片を鑑賞者に強烈な視覚的インパクトをもって突き付けるところに一脈相通じるものがあるように感じられたのです。

三島さんの代表作と自他ともに認める《20世紀の記憶》は、空き缶作品をはじめとする従来の三島作品に顕著な遊び心やユーモアは影を潜め、むしろシリアスさが際立っています。とはいえ《20世紀の記憶》は、割れやすい反面永続性のある陶を印刷物と組み合わせ、情報の問題を再認識させるという三島作品の基軸に則ったものであり、さらには近場で手に入ったゴミとしての中古のレンガを再利用している点からも、作者が長く追い求めてきた表現世界のひとつの帰結点がここにあり、一見すると従来の三島作品とは趣を異にしているものの、逆にもっとも三島さんらしい作品と言えるのかもしれません。

ともあれ城南島で拝見して以来高じていた、より多くの方々にこの強靭な作品と今一度向き合っていただきたいという強い思いは、今回ようやく実現の運びとなったわけですが、練馬区立美術館での展示は、ややチャレンジングなものとなりました。というのは、《20世紀の記憶》は1984年頃から制作が始まり、数次にわたる部分的展示を経て、2013年にART FACTORY城南島において作品が完成すると、サイズはますます巨大化して移動は困難となり、それ以降は同地で常設展示が続けられてきたからです。このたび同施設を運営する株式会社東横イン/株式会社ギャラリー1045のご厚意を賜り、また当館スタッフの奮闘もあって、初めて城南島の地を離れ当館にてフルスケールによる展示が行なわれることになりました。

21世紀も四半世紀が経過しようとしている昨今、世界はいまだに戦禍が絶えず、前世紀の歴史から多くを学んだはずであるにもかかわらず、負の遺産を引きずってしまっているかのように見えます。「死んだものを未来に対する「希望(ホープ)」の、その礎として生きかえらせるのが歴史というものなのだ」[2]と小説家の堀田善衞はかつてインドへの旅のさなかに記しましたが、私たちは今こそこの三島作品と改めて向かい合い、共鳴することで、彼女が作品に刻印した歴史の記憶を、来るべき未来への記憶として受け止められないだろうかと考え、当館では《20世紀の記憶》を中心に展覧会を構成することとしました。

並行して、三島さんが美術家として最初に取り組んだ絵画にも着目し、1950年代の具象画から抽象画、60年代の印刷物を用いたコラージュ作品及びシルクスクリーンの技法を取り入れた平面作品を一堂に展示します。特に新聞やチラシなどの印刷物をコラージュして彩色した絵画は、第31回独立展の独立賞・須田賞(1963年)、第9回シェル美術賞展佳作賞(1965年)を受賞するなど当時高い評価を得ていたにもかかわらず、三島さん自身は「なんかもう一つ迫力ないな」[3]と物足りなさを感じていたようです。比較的短いスパンで絵画のスタイルを次々に変えていったのは、当時の美術動向へのセンシティブな反応というよりはむしろ、自身の絵画に飽き足らず、緊張感や現実感、迫力を注入しようと日々模索していたことが背景にあったと思われます。「何気なく新聞を見てるうちに、小さくても立体ってえらく存在感があるなあと感じた。新聞割れたら面白いなあとふと思ったんですね。そこには不安感もあるし」。[4]

70年代に入ると三島さんは、絵画から陶による立体作品へと表現媒体の転換をはかります。絵画の制作では夫で抽象画家の三島茂司の存在がありましたが、陶芸では専門的な手ほどきを受けずに独力で創作に臨みました。その結果、伝統的な手法にとらわれることなく、わずか1年半ほどで日本陶芸展の前衛部門に入選を果たし、陶芸界を驚かせています。土を紙のように薄く伸ばし、陶土の表面に新聞やチラシの文字をシルクスクリーンで転写し焼成する技法によって生み出された立体作品を、三島さんは「割れる印刷物」と称し、独自のスタイルとして確立させたのです。いつ割れるかしれない陶による印刷物を模したオブジェには、情報洪水の中で埋没する不安感や恐怖感が表現されています。そして新聞やチラシをはじめ、コミック、パッケージ、フィルム、段ボール、飲料ボトルなど日々の暮らしの品々が次々と三島さんの手によって陶によるオブジェと化し、その最良の成果が本展には集められました。こうした多様な陶のオブジェのほか、後に続く大型インスタレーション作品もまた、三島さんが絵画で用いたシルクスクリーンによる転写の技法がベースの部分で用いられており、媒体は変われども三島さんの創作は、その基底において一貫してつながっていることが判ります。

加えて本展では、作品素材として産業廃棄物を高温処理した溶融スラグを使った作品や、自ら収集した廃材や鉄くずなどを取り込んだ近年の作品も展示します。情報からゴミへと問題意識を次第に移していった三島さんは、長年にわたって制作に使ってきた陶土も有限の資源と聞くと、溶融スラグの使用を思い立つなど素材に対しても執着することなく、自分が表現したい世界にもっとも適した素材をその都度選び取り、試行錯誤を繰り返して作品作りに邁進してきました。三島さんのドライなまでの素材への拘りのなさは、創作の自由度をより広げるひとつの要因となったと言えるでしょう。

「私は陶芸家でなくて現代美術家」と三島さんは常々言ってはばからないものの、印刷物を立体化した陶による作品が注目を集めるあまり、これまで三島さんは前衛陶芸家としてのイメージが広く定着してきました。今でこそ現代アートの工芸化、工芸の現代アート化により、両者はますます近接してジャンルを隔てる垣根も低くなっていますが、かつての前衛陶芸家としての固定化した見方は、三島さんの現代美術家としての正当な評価をこれまで妨げてきたように思います。本展に出品されている初期の絵画作品が再び注目を集めるようになったのは近年のことであり、これまで絵画と陶による作品は確かな連続性があるにもかかわらず、並列して展示される機会もごく限られていました。70年にわたる長いキャリアを誇りながら、三島さんの美術館での個展開催は、意外なことに昨年実施された岐阜県現代陶芸美術館における展覧会を待たねばならなかったのです。

三島さんが絵画に取り組んだ時期は、日本美術界にアンフォルメル旋風が巻き起こった時代であり、また彼女が暮らし、制作の舞台ともなった大阪は、日本を代表する前衛美術グループ、具体美術協会の拠点の一つでありました。さらには、同時代に京都では走泥社による前衛陶芸の活動も展開されました。こうした日本の戦後前衛美術の大きなうねりの中で、三島さんは団体展への出品を除きいずれのグループにも属さず、「いつも生活している中で、あっ、これ面白いなと思ったものをパッと実現させて、作品にしてしまう」(5)スタイルで、ユーモアを忘れずに独自の制作を展開してきました。情報化社会や大量消費社会へ厳しい視線を投げかけつつも、情報やゴミを異化作用を通して造形表現へと転化させた三島作品をどのように再評価し、日本の戦後美術のなかに位置づけうるのか、本展の開催がその検証を促すひとつの契機となることを願っています。また多くの鑑賞者の皆さまに三島作品の魅力にふれていただき、とりわけ《20世紀の記憶》からは何かを感じ、考え、不透明な未来に向けての何かしらのヒントをここから持ち帰っていただけるならば、これに勝る喜びはございません。

最後になりましたが、本展の開催にあたり当館の様々な要望に応じてくださった三島喜美代さん並びに女婿の上田準三さんに、改めて心より御礼申し上げます。また、本書にご寄稿くださった森村泰昌さん、徳山拓一さんに深甚なる謝意を表します。

（練馬区立美術館 館長）

註

1 コンセプチュアル・アーティスト、ハンス・ハーケによるサイトスペシフィック・インスタレーション。会場となったヴェネチアのドイツ館は、ナチス政権下の1938年、古典主義様式により再建された建物。ハーケは、入口に1990（ドイツが再統一された年）の年号の入った1ドイツマルク貨幣、正面の壁にヒトラーがドイツ館を視察した折の写真を掲げ、対面の壁に「ゲルマニア」の文字を刷り込んだ。さらに大理石の床を破壊、その上を観客が歩くと高い天井の館内に乾いた音が木霊した。ナチスへの批判と、再統一後のドイツの再生を表象した作品として高い評価を得た。

2 堀田善衛『インドで考えたこと』岩波書店、1957年、210頁

3 森村泰昌「野にありて跳べ　美の活動家に会いに行く―三島喜美代」『日経回廊』日本経済新聞社、2016年10月号、108頁

4 同上

5 ハンス・ウルリッヒ・オブリストによるインタビュー「三島喜美代は語る」『三島喜美代―Kimiyo Mishima』艸居、2021年、105頁

Memories for the Future: On the Mishima Kimiyo Exhibition

Ito Masanobu

The Nerima Art Museum is truly delighted to present a retrospective exhibition of the contemporary artist Mishima Kimiyo, whose star has been rapidly rising both in Japan and abroad in recent years. As this is Mishima's first solo exhibition at a museum in Tokyo, rather than focusing on recent works, a deliberate decision was made to trace her entire career, from the early paintings, through her ceramic sculpture series of "breakable printed matter" and her monumental installation *Memories of the 20th Century* (1984–2013, no. 82) to her most recent projects. Through this exhibition, we aim to showcase Mishima's extraordinary practice and her consistent focus, over the course of her 70-year creative arc, on societal realities such as information saturation and the massive volumes of waste we produce.

I first met Mishima in January 2017. This was when I visited Art Factory Jonanjima in Ota-ku, Tokyo to request the inclusion of her ceramic work depicting empty beverage cans, during preparations for *The Superlative Artistry of Japan*, an overseas touring exhibition organized by the Japan Foundation. In this work, the cans appear to have been casually tossed into a wastebasket, and each one is crafted with such meticulous detail that they indeed epitomize "superlative artistry." The ceramic surfaces, silkscreened with text and hand-painted in vibrant Pop colors, thoroughly conceal the nature of the material, leading viewers to nearly miss the fact that the "cans" are crafted from ceramic. Upon closer inspection and recognition, this discovery elicits astonishment and irrepressible smiles. I immediately asked Mishima to present the work in the exhibition, to which she graciously consented.

However, my most stunning experience that day was viewing Mishima's largest installation, *Memories of the 20th Century*, on view in the current exhibition. Filling a space exceeding 20 by 10 meters, this work is not only monumental in scale but also enormously dense, generating palpable tension that pervades the space. Encountering this silent world where it seemed as if time had frozen, I too was stricken silent with amazement. I could hardly believe that the delicate artist with whom I had just been speaking had produced this massive installation, which was clearly a labor of immense dedication.

Memories of the 20th Century covers the floor with approximately 10,600 fireproof bricks, their surfaces silkscreened with newspaper articles and other materials that Mishima selected from across the 20th century. She describes the act of transferring information from printed matter to ceramic objects as "fossilization of information." This work serves as a tangible representation of the 20th century's unfathomably vast volume of information, and I believe it also embodies Mishima's personal memories of and reflections on that era. The bricks feature Japanese newspaper articles on one side and foreign-language articles on the other, with topics ranging from the Anglo-Japanese Alliance and the moon landing to Tonegawa Susumu's winning the Nobel Prize and E. coli O157 outbreaks. Despite the lack of focus on any one theme, words connoting war inevitably catch the eye, implying that the century was profoundly scarred by conflict from beginning to end. The repurposed old bricks were previously used at kilns in Toki City, Gifu Prefecture, and many are chipped or discolored, their unevenness giving the entire space a disquieting atmosphere. The vista formed by these more than 10,000 bricks evokes an apocalyptic science-fictional world at the endpoint of an information-overloaded society, no doubt evoking the ruins of a bombed-out city to some viewers. The installation maintains its silence while emanating an indescribable presence.

I found myself reminded of Hans Haacke's installation Germania, which I viewed at the German Pavilion during the 1993 Venice Biennale.[1] This work displayed, facing the main entrance, a photograph of Hitler inspecting the pavilion in 1934, and it involved breaking the marble floor, rebuilt during the Nazi regime, and having visitors walk on it, making it a site-specific as well as an interactive work. In this sense it differs from *Memories of the 20th Century*, which is not bound to a specific site and instead transforms the existing space wherever it is installed. Also, while *Germania* delivers the thrust of its message efficiently without time-consuming processes, *Memories of the 20th Century* entails a massive, even excessive accumulation of bricks, achieving an overwhelming effect through sheer volume. In this regard, the two works might be seen as contrasting. At the same time, they were produced almost concurrently, and both present scenes reminiscent of ruins and make a stunning impact on viewers through fragments of history, which to me indicates a shared underlying theme.

Memories of the 20th Century is widely acknowledged, including by Mishima herself, as the artist's magnum opus. It departs from the playful humor that characterized her other works such as the empty cans, and instead is marked by deep seriousness. However, it stays true to the essence of Mishima's practice by fusing fragile yet long-lasting ceramics with printed matter to reexamine issues of information saturation. Also, the repurposing of old used bricks, previously abandoned, which she acquired in her neighborhood, reconnects with the creative territory that Mishima has explored over the decades. On first glance it might appear quite different from her other works, yet paradoxically, it might also be regarded as the most emblematic of her oeuvre.

Ever since my visit to Jonanjima, I have only grown more eager for wider audiences to engage with this formidable installation. Now this wish has finally come to fruition, though exhibiting it at the Nerima Art Museum presented its challenges. This was because production of *Memories of the 20th Century* began around 1984 and, after several exhibitions in a partial state, it was completed in 2013 at Art Factory Jonanjima. The work had significantly increased in size, rendering it difficult to transport, and it has been on permanent view there ever since. Thanks to the generosity of Toyoko Inn Co., Ltd., and Gallery 1045 Co., Ltd., which manage the facility, and the dedication of our museum staff, we are now able to present the work in its entirety at our venue, marking its first departure from Jonanjima.

As we edge closer to a quarter of the way through the 21st century, the world remains mired in conflict. It seems that rather than learning the lessons of the previous century, we continue to be shadowed by its dark legacy. During travels in India in 1956-57, the novelist Hotta Yoshie wrote that "History is the resurrection of the dead as a foundation for 'hope' for the future."[2] With this in mind, I believe it is time to confront Mishima's work anew, to let it resonate, and to interpret the histories she embedded in her work as memories for the future. For this reason, the museum has chosen to structure this exhibition around *Memories of the 20th Century*.

Meanwhile, we also highlight the paintings that were Mishima's entry point as an artist, presenting a lineup that ranges from figurative paintings of the 1950s to abstract works, and includes pieces from the 1960s incorporating collage and later applying silkscreen. Notably, her paintings featuring collages of printed matter such as newspapers and flyers earned accolades such as the Dokuritsu Prize and the Suda Prize at the 31st Dokuritsu Exhibition (1963) and an honorable mention at the 9th Annual Shell Exhibition (1965), but Mishima was dissatisfied, feeling that "they lack impact."[3] Her rapid changes in painting style during a relatively short time seem to have been driven not so much by sensitive reactions to current art developments as by her tireless quest to imbue her paintings with tension, actuality, and intensity. She recalled: "When I was casually looking at the newspaper, it struck me that even if they're small, three-dimensional objects have a remarkable presence. I thought it would be intriguing if a newspaper was breakable. It also gave me a sense of anxiety."[4]

As the 1970s dawned, Mishima transitioned from painting to three-dimensional ceramic works. While her husband, the abstract painter Mishima Shigeji, no doubt influenced her painting, in the medium of ceramics she did not undergo formal training and took a thoroughly original approach to her art. As a result, she was unfettered by traditional techniques, and after just about a year and a half, she had her work selected for the avant-garde category of the Japan Ceramic Art Exhibition in 1971 and was astonishing the ceramics world. By flattening clay to paper-like thinness and transferring text from newspapers and flyers onto its surface by silkscreen before firing, Mishima created three-dimensional works that she described as "breakable printed matter" and established her own singular style. The ceramic objects mimicking printed matter could break at any moment, and express a sense of anxiety and dread submerged in a flood of excessive information.She reimagined items from everyday life such as newspapers and flyers, as well as comics, packaging, film, cardboard, and beverage bottles, as numerous superbly crafted ceramic objects, culminating in masterworks which we are proud to feature in this exhibition. She applied the silkscreen transfer technique used in her paintings not only to these diverse ceramic objects but also to her later large-scale installations, illustrating an underlying, unbroken through-line connecting her practice regardless of changes in media. Also, this exhibition presents recent works made with molten slag (a material created by melting down industrial waste at high temperatures) or incorporating discarded materials and scrap metal that she personally gathered. In gradually shifting her focus from information to garbage, Mishima has ceased limiting herself to clay, her longtime material, having recognized that clay was a finite resource. Recently, she selects whichever materials best articulate her vision for each work, and applies trial and error to the prolific production of a diverse oeuvre. The sangfroid of Mishima's detachment from specific materials has further expanded the scope of her free-ranging creative expression.

Although Mishima has frequently stated that she is not a ceramicist but a contemporary artist, her ceramic works transforming printed matter into three-dimensional art objects drew such attention that they cemented her reputation as an avant-garde ceramicist. In the current era, with contemporary art drawing closer to crafts and vice versa, distinctions between fields are becoming increasingly blurred in Japan. However, the persistent view of Mishima as primarily an avant-garde ceramicist may have overshadowed the recognition she deserves as a contemporary artist. Despite the evident continuity between her paintings and ceramic works, they have seldom been exhibited together, and the renewed attention to her early paintings, as in this exhibition, is only a recent phenomenon. It is astounding that while her remarkable career spans seven decades, Mishima did not have a solo museum exhibition until last year's show at the Museum of Modern Ceramic Art, Gifu.

Mishima began painting during a time when the influence of European Art Informel dominated the Japanese art scene. Osaka, the city where she lived and worked, was one of the bases of operation of Gutai, Japan's preeminent avant-garde art group, while around the same time the avant-garde ceramics group Sodeisha was active in Kyoto. Amid these major postwar Japanese avant-garde movements, Mishima refrained from joining any specific circle, limiting her involvement to participating in group exhibitions, and pursued her distinctive style, always imbued with humor, in such a way that, in her words, she could "swiftly bring to life any intriguing idea that suddenly struck me in the course of day-to-day life."[5] While casting a critical gaze on our society of information saturation and mass consumption, she transmutes both information and garbage into art, and we are eager to see how this exhibition will contribute to further research on and reappraisal of her truly unique position within the context of postwar Japanese art. Nothing would make us happier than to see visitors engage with Mishima's remarkable works, particularly drawing insights from *Memories of the 20th Century*, reflecting on them, and possibly finding clues for navigating our uncertain future.

In closing, I would like to reiterate our heartfelt gratitude to Mishima Kimiyo and her son-in-law Ueda Junzo for meeting the museum's many requests related to this exhibition. We are also deeply thankful to Morimura Yasumasa and Tokuyama Hirokazu for their contributions to this catalogue.

Director, Nerima Art Museum

Notes

1. *Germania* is a site-specific installation by the conceptual artist Hans Haacke. The venue, the German Pavilion in Venice, was reconstructed in a neoclassical style under the Nazi regime in 1938. Haacke placed a one-Deutsche Mark coin dating from 1990 (the year Germany was reunified) at the entrance, and on the wall facing the entrance he displayed a photo of Hitler inspecting the pavilion. The word Germania was printed on the wall across from it. The marble floor was shattered, and as visitors walked over it, their steps echoed in the high-ceilinged hall. The work was highly praised as a condemnation of the Nazis and a representation of the post-unification rebirth of Germany.
2. Hotta Yoshie, *Indo de kangaeta koto* [Thoughts in India], Iwanami Shoten, 1957, p. 210.
3. Morimura Yasumasa, "*No ni arite tobe: bi no katsudoka ni ai ni iku*" [Leap into the Wild: Meetings with Aesthetic Activists], *Nikkei kairo*, no. 10, Nikkei Inc., 2016, p. 108.
4. Ibid.
5. Interview with Hans Ulrich Obrist, "Mishima Kimiyo Speaks," *Mishima Kimiyo*, Sokyo Gallery, 2021, p. 105.

凡例

・本書は「三島喜美代ー未来への記憶」展の図録として制作された。
・第1章 初期作品 1950年代～1970年頃、第2章 割れる印刷物 1970年頃～、第3章 ゴミと向き合う、第4章 大型インスタレーションで構成される。
・展覧会会場での展示順は、かならずしも本書掲載順と一致しない。
・作品番号は各章ごとに制作年順に従った。なお、文中で出品作品を示す場合(no.番号)とした。
・作品番号は巻末の作品リストと一致するが、掲載順はかならずしも番号順ではない。
・図版ページの作品データは作品名(和・英)、制作年、所蔵の順で記載している。技法・素材、サイズなどの情報については、巻末の作品リストに記載している。個人蔵については、所蔵を空欄としている。
・章解説は、伊東正伸(練馬区立美術館館長)が執筆した。
・翻訳は、クリストファー・スティヴンズ(pp. 16-22, 27-29, 35-39, p. 43, pp. 78-79, p. 83, 137, 159)、アンドレアス・シュトゥールマン(p. 7, 40, pp. 185-89)による。
・「参考 大型インスタレーションおよびパブリックアート」を資料として掲載した。
—作品データは、作品名、制作年、素材・技法、サイズ、所蔵先の順で記載している(和・英)。

Notes

・This book serves as a catalogue for the exhibition "Mishima Kimiyo: Memories for the Future."
・Contents are divided into four chapters: 1. The Early Years: 1950s – c. 1970 / 2. Breakable Printed Matter: Circa 1970 Onward / 3. Grappling with Garbage / 4. Large-Scale Installations
・Works featured in this book do not necessarily appear in the order of display at the exhibition.
・Works are numbered in the order of their creation in each chapter, and indicated in the text as "no. XX."
・Numbers of artworks are consistent with the List of Works at the end of the book, however featured works do not necessarily appear in numerical order.
・Captions of images in the book include (in order) the following information: Title of work (Jap/Eng), year of creation, owner/collection. For materials/techniques, sizes and other information, please refer to the List of Works at the end of the book. Private owners of artworks are not named.
・Introductory texts for each chapter written by Ito Masanobu (Director of the Nerima Art Museum).
・Texts translated into English by Christopher Stephens (pp. 16-22, 27-29, 35-39, p. 43, pp. 78-79, p. 83, 137, 159) and Andreas Stuhlmann (p. 7, 40, pp. 185-89).
・"Large-scale Installations and Public Art" are included for reference.
Works data appear in the following order (in Japanese and English): title, year of creation, material and technique, dimensions, collection.
・Japanese names appear in the surname followed by given name order.

1

初期作品
1950年代～1970年頃

The Early Years:
1950s – c.1970

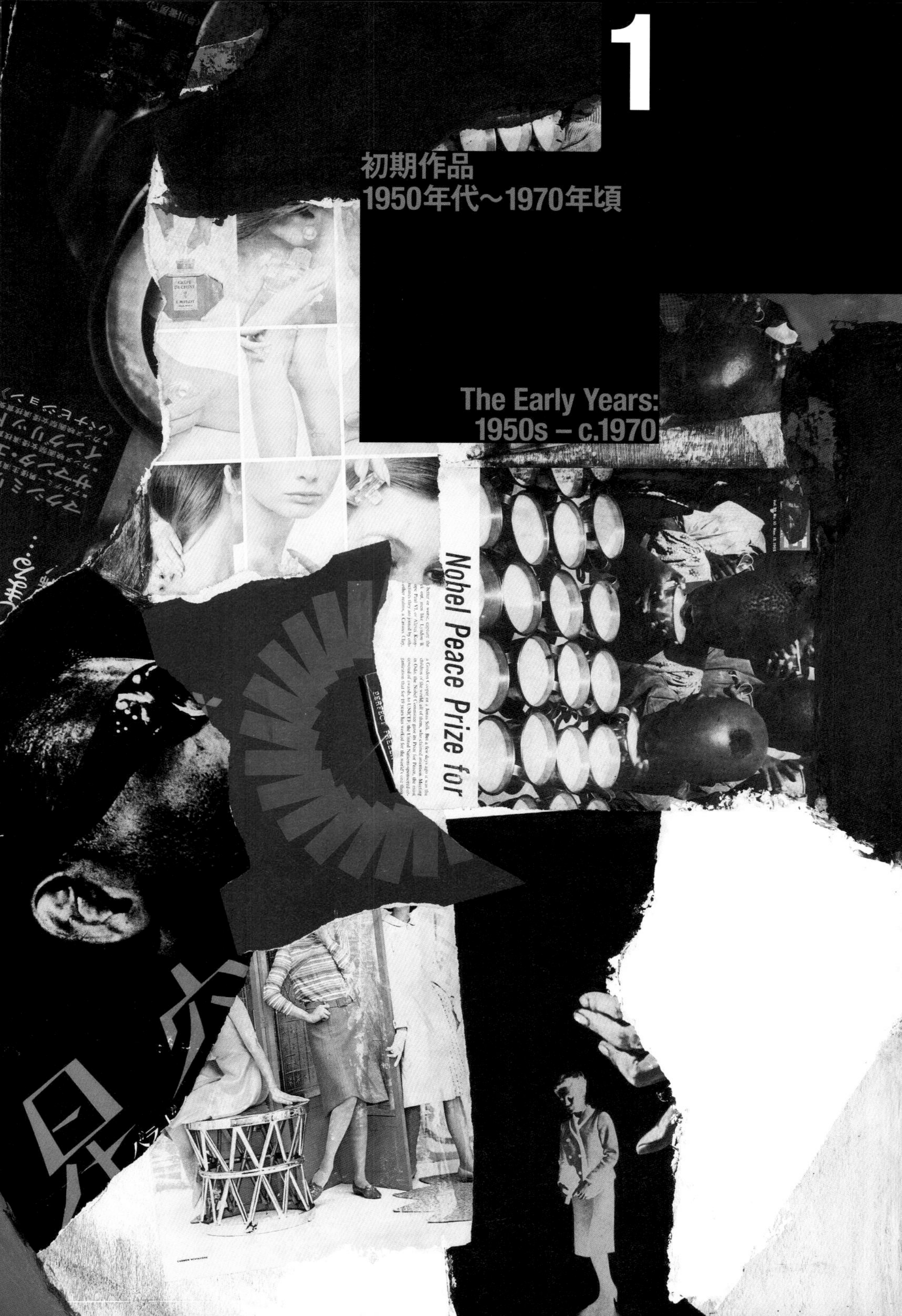

第1章　初期作品　1950年代〜1970年頃

三島喜美代は、1950年代に絵画を出発点に現代美術家としての活動をスタートさせた。同時期に日本を席捲していたアンフォルメル風の抽象絵画の影響を受けながらも、早くからコラージュによる油彩画に取り組んでいる。画面に貼り付けられたのは『Life』や海外の新聞など情報化社会の中で消費された印刷物、あるいは復員した義兄が持ち帰った毛布など用を終えて身近にあったものだった。当時の絵画《Work-64-I》(no. 9)は、「現代美術の動向　絵画と彫塑」展(京都国立近代美術館、1964年)の出品作品に選出され、また《夜の詩I》は「第9回シェル美術賞展」(1965年)佳作賞を受賞するなど高い評価を得ていた。1960年代半ばからはシルクスクリーンによる転写を取り入れ、そこに描画を加えてポップ・アート的な展開もみせている(nos. 14, 17, 18)。だが三島は自身の絵画にもう一つ迫力がない、緊張感がないと感じていたという。

「何気なく新聞を見ているうちに、小さくても立体って、えらく存在感があると感じた。新聞、割れたら面白いなとふと思ったんですね。そこには不安感もあるし」。*

三島の目にとまったのは、くしゃくしゃになった新聞紙。これを陶で作ったらどうなるか、触れたら割れるかもしれないという緊張感も醸し出すのではないか。三島は1970年頃には、新聞や雑誌などの印刷物を陶を使って立体化する試みを独学で始めた。三島の代名詞となる作品群「割れる印刷物」の誕生である。

*森村泰昌「野にありて跳べ　美の活動家に会いに行く」『日経回廊』2016年第10号

1. The Early Years: 1950s – c. 1970

Mishima Kimiyo began her career as a contemporary artist in the 1950s, initially as a painter. While influenced by the Art Informel-style abstraction prevalent in Japan during this era, she soon began incorporating collage into her oil paintings. The materials she affixed to her surfaces ranged from printed matter indicative of the burgeoning information society, such as pages from *Life* magazine and overseas newspapers that she happened to find nearby, to items imbued with personal history, such as blankets her brother-in-law brought home when returning from military service. Her work was highly acclaimed, with her painting *Work-64-I* (no. 9) selected for the *Trends in Contemporary Japanese Art: Painting and Sculpture* exhibition at the National Museum of Modern Art, Kyoto in 1964, and *Poem of Night I* winning an honorable mention at the 9th Shell Art Award Exhibition in 1965. In the mid-1960s, Mishima ventured in a Pop Art direction, applying silkscreen transfers to her works and then adding to them by hand (nos. 14, 17, 18). However, Mishima says she perceived a lack of intensity and tension in her paintings.

"When I was casually looking at a newspaper, it struck me that even if they're small, three-dimensional objects have a remarkable presence. I thought it would be intriguing if a newspaper was breakable. It also gave me a sense of anxiety."*

Mishima's eye fell upon a crumpled-up newspaper. She thought about what it would be like to render this in ceramic, imbuing the piece with a sense of tension in that touching it might cause it to break. Around 1970, Mishima independently explored the conversion of printed matter such as newspapers and magazines into three-dimensional ceramic forms. This led to creation of the "breakable printed matter" series which is synonymous with her oeuvre.

* Morimura Yasumasa, "No ni arite tobe: bi no katsudoka ni ai ni iku" [Leap into the Wild: Meetings with Aesthetic Activists], *Nikkei kairo*, no. 10, 2016.

1
マスカット
Muscats
1951年

2
かぼちゃ
Pumpkin
1952年

3
作品B
Work B
1952年

4
スケッチカード
Sketch Cards
1957年

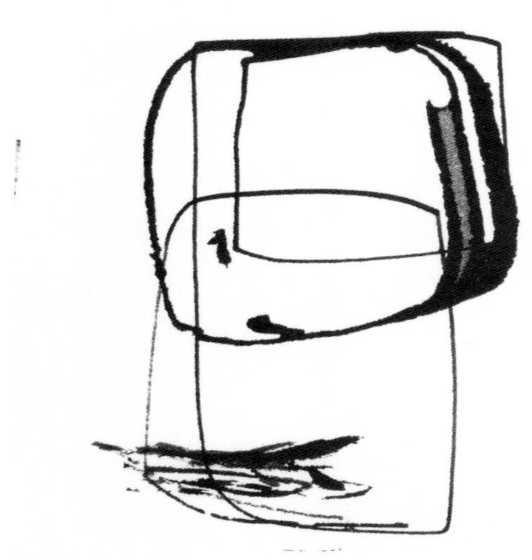

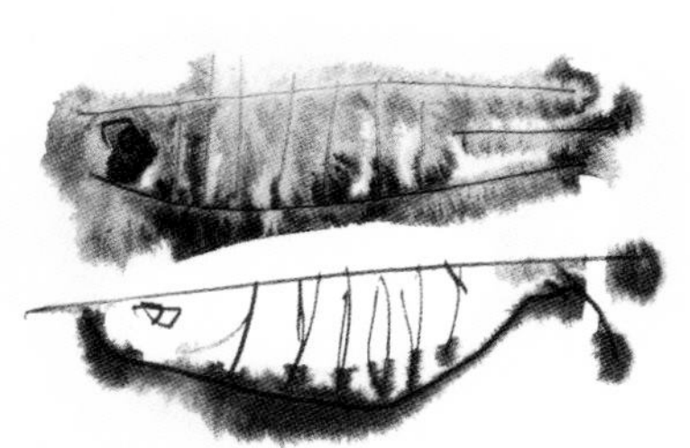

5-1
Untitled
1957年

5-2
Untitled
1957年

6
スケッチブック
Sketchbook
1957年

7
覇
Ascendancy
1960年

dren
-card sales
Nobel Peace Prize
better or worse, capture the
ek out, men like Lyndon B.
ope Paul VI, or Alexei Kosy-
netimes they are joined by oth-
other realms, a Cassius Clay,
a Gordon Cooper or a Jonas Salk. But a few
children of the world, all of them, who claimed
in Oslo, the Nobel Committee gave its Prize
coveted of awards, to UNICEF, the United Na
ganization that for 19 years has worked for the
PERFECT

8
Work 60-B
1960年
美術資料センター株式会社

9
Work-64-I
1964年
京都国立近代美術館

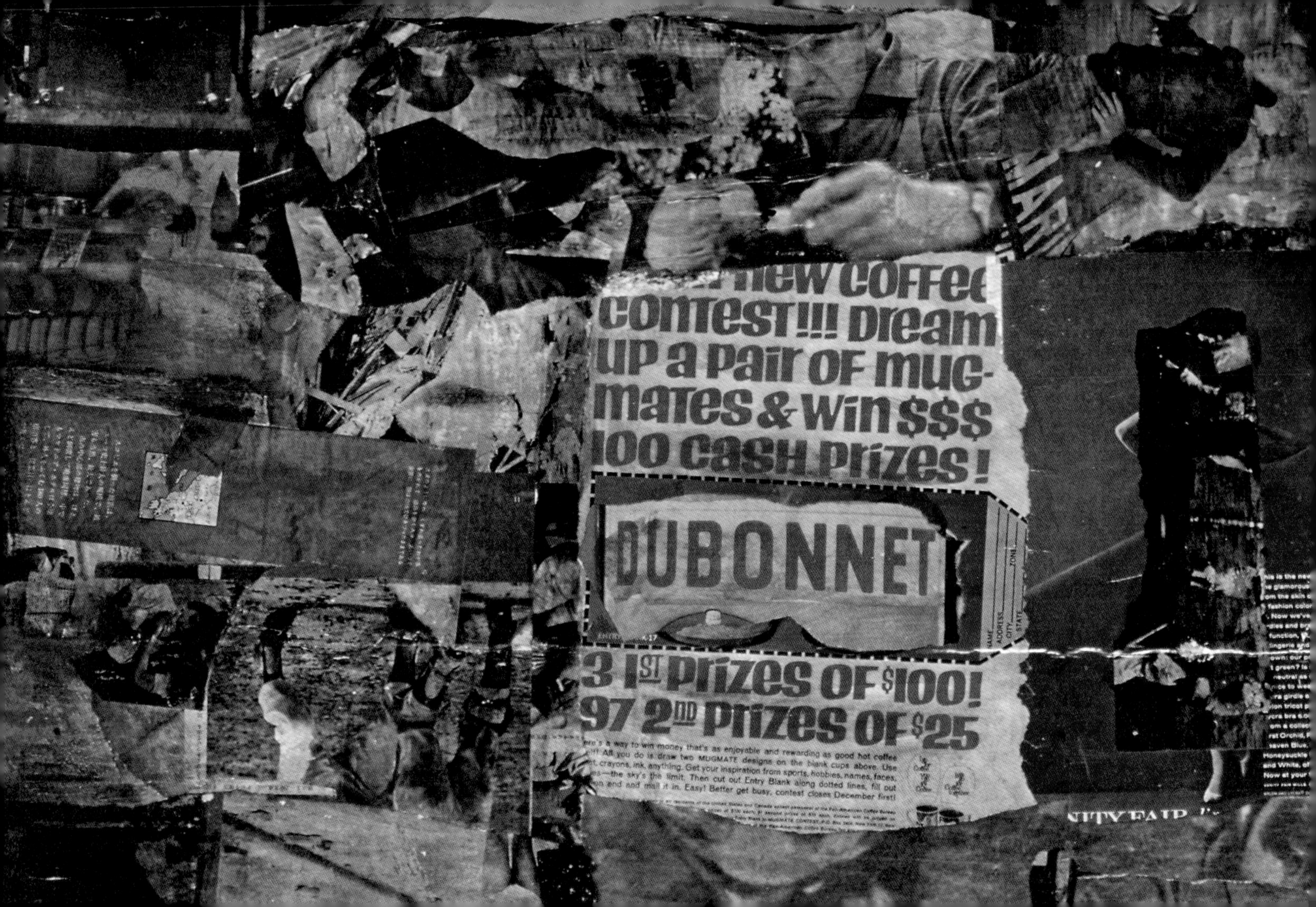
new coffee
contest!!! Dream
up a pair of mug-
mates & win $$$
100 cash prizes!
DUBONNET
3 1st prizes of $100!
97 2nd prizes of $25

Loi Beats Manca
6 Workers Injured
As Boiler Explodes
US Plans To Sell
Bonds In Europe
PAPILLOTES
College Ace mini
RETIREMENT
Mexico Way

10
Work 64-III
1964年

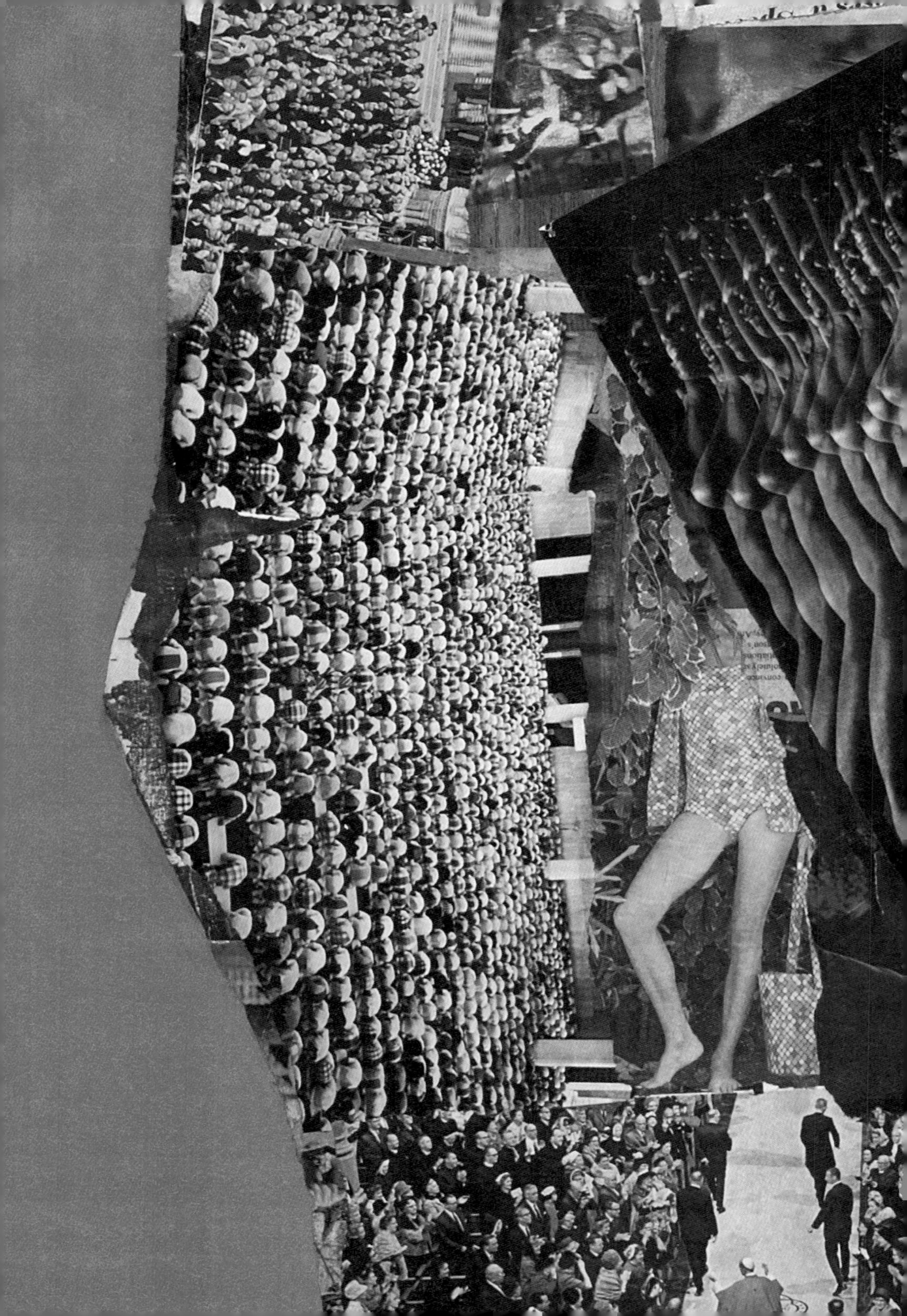

11
作品 65-H
Work 65-H
1965年

12
変貌III
Transfiguration III
1966年
美術資料センター株式会社

WE SUPPORT —
DAVE SCOTT
SENATOR
55TH DISTRICT
riot ended in rubble.
Today, Watts smolders on . . .
SEE NEXT PAGE
Colin Davis
Istvan Kertesz
JAZZ VOCAL SERIES
Odeon

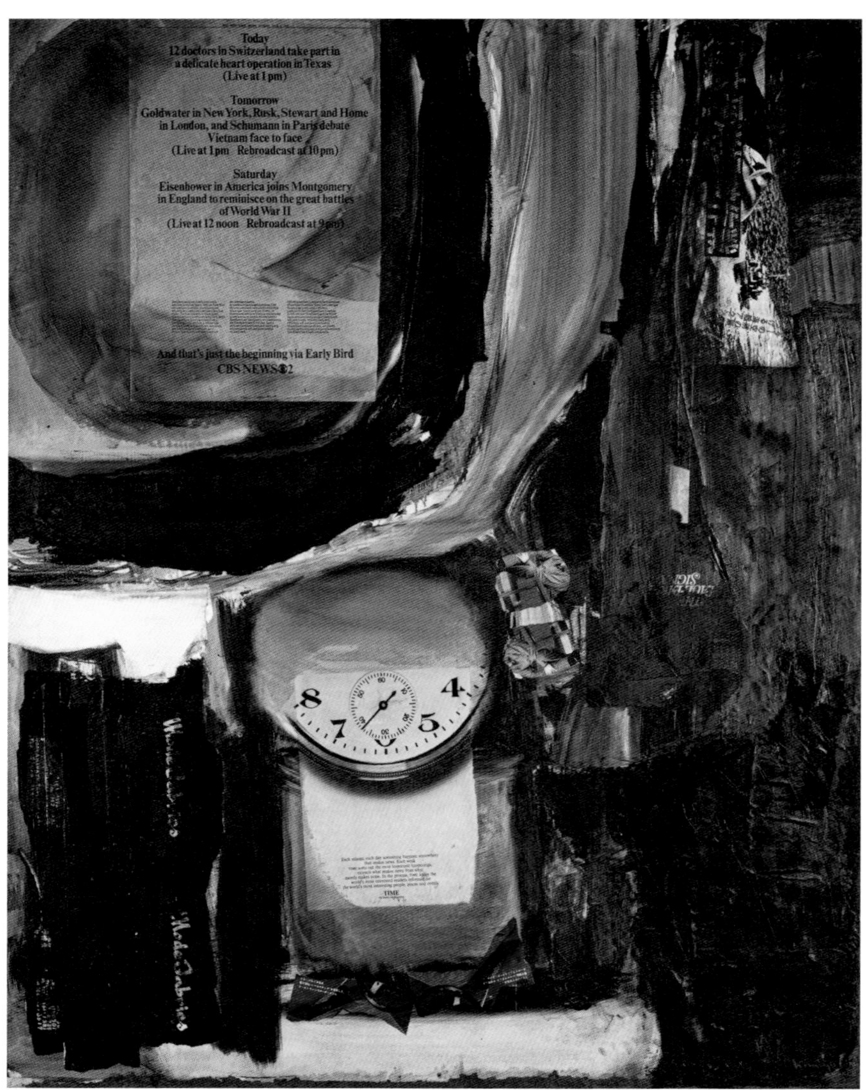

13
断章III
Morceau III
1966年
京都国立近代美術館

16
作品F
Work F
1969年

15
作品 68-A
Work 68-A
1968年

Starting
October 1,
we have
a place
in
the sun
BRASIL '66
トーヨー
ジエッ

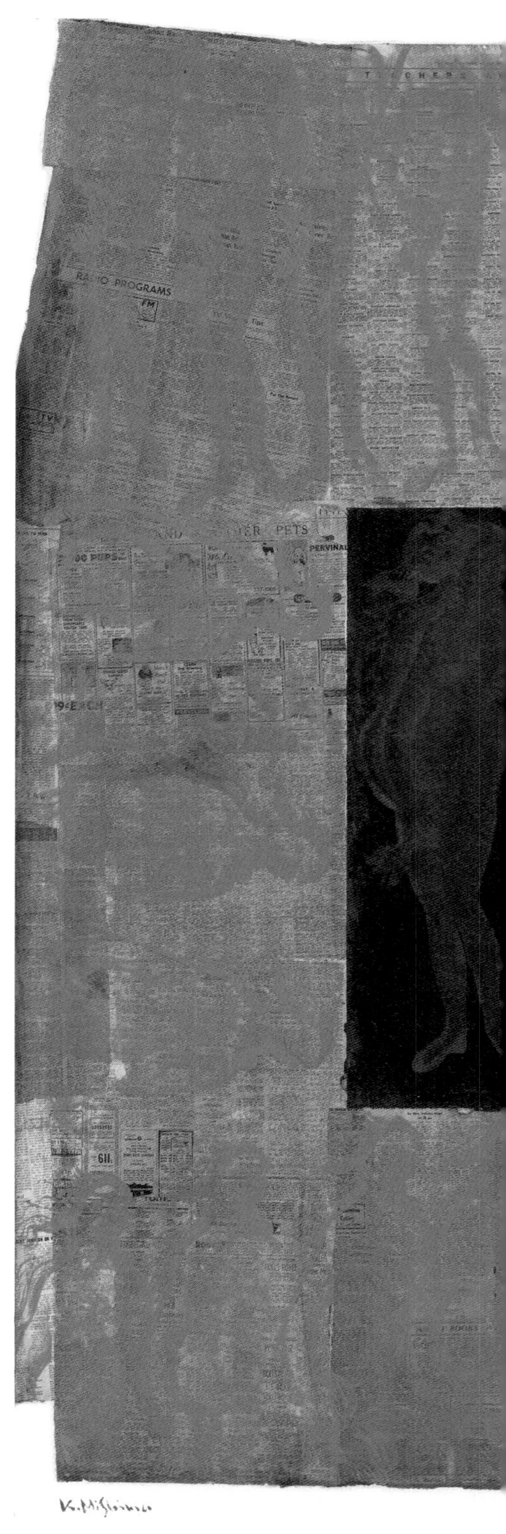

14
ヴィーナスの変貌 V
Transfiguration of Venus V
1967年

Diplomatic Ties With US
France, Russia

17
Untitled
1970年

18
Untitled
1970-71年

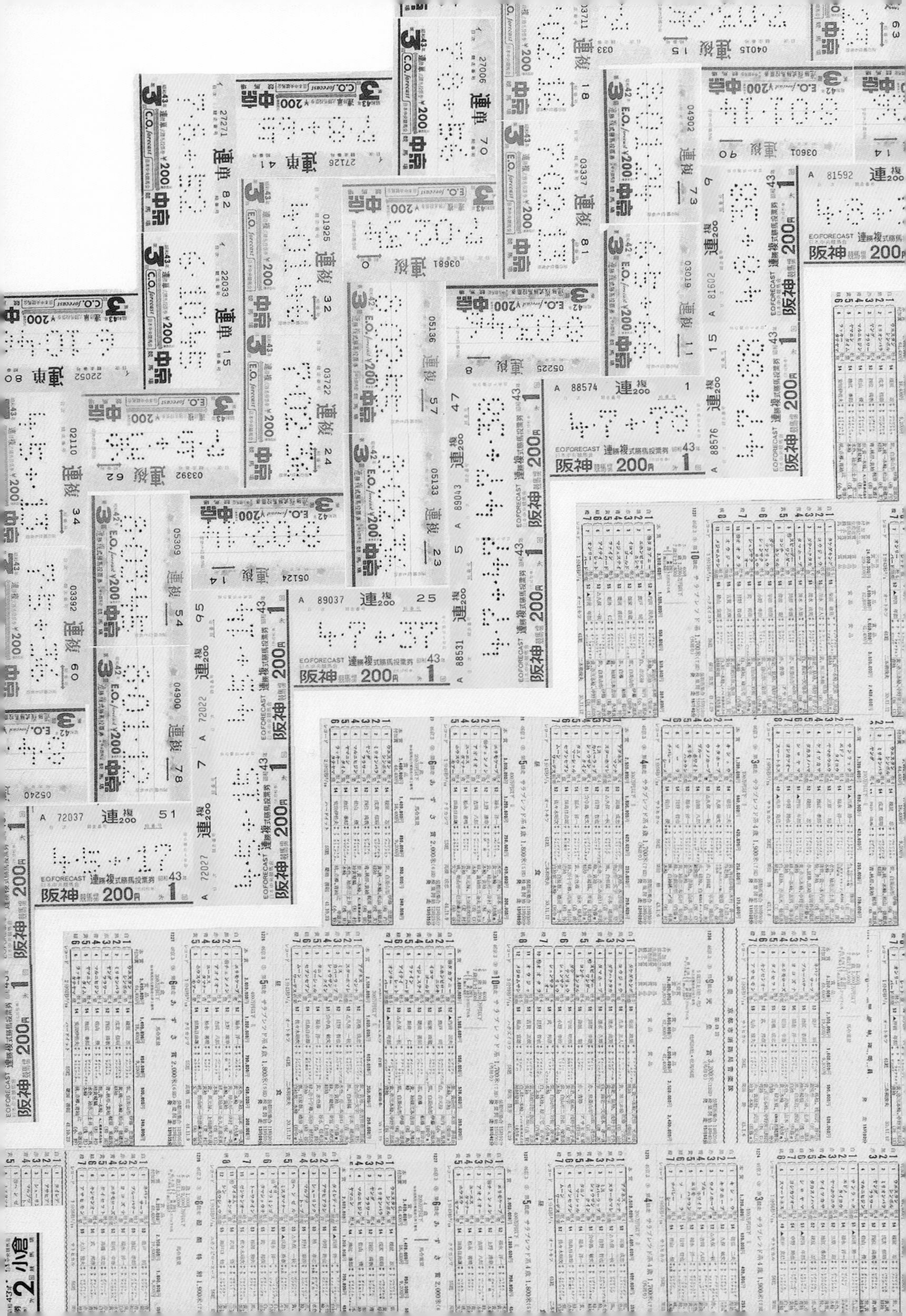

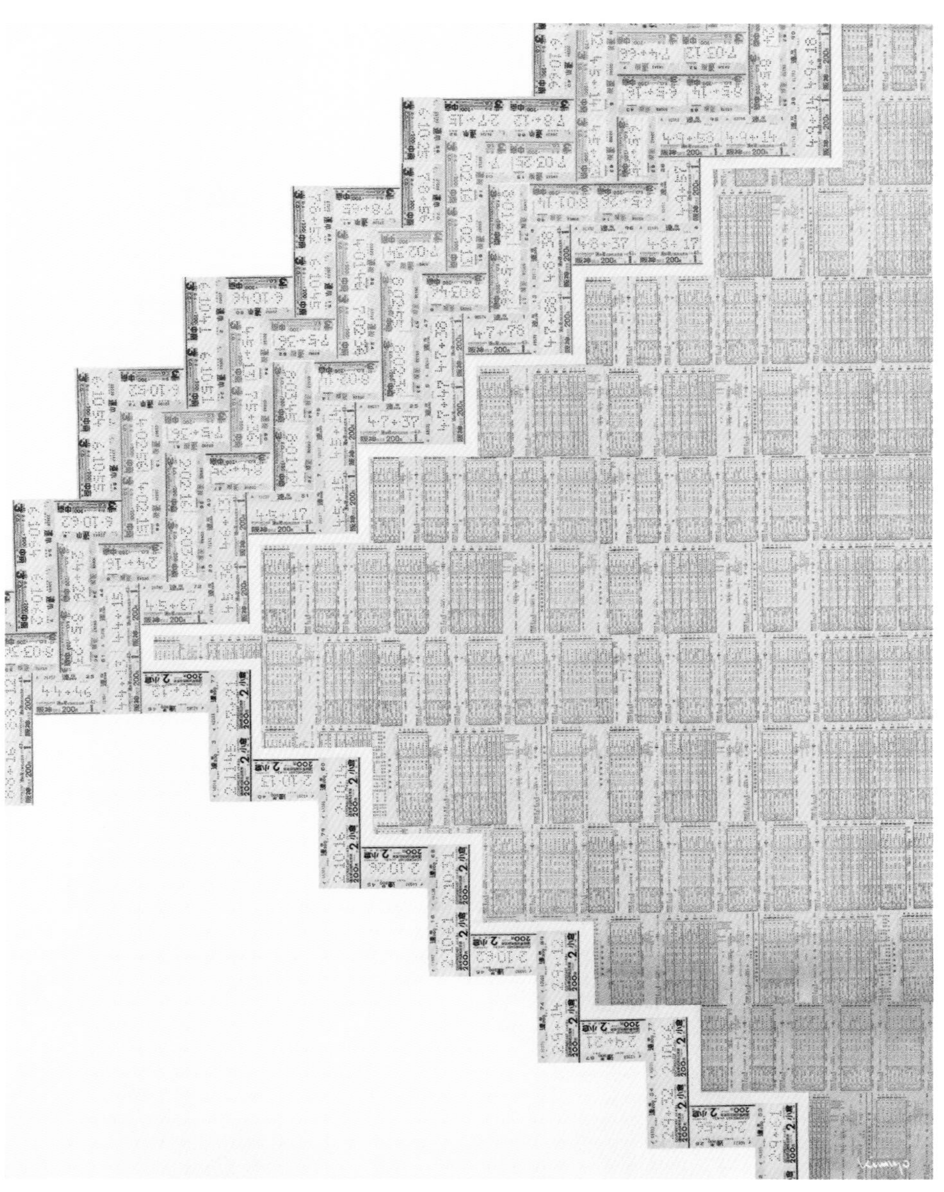

19
メモリー III
Memory III
1971年

三島喜美代と1960～1970年代初頭の印刷物：コラージュ、シルクスクリーンの題材に選ばれたもの

新井晃

1960年代初め、三島喜美代は油彩画にコラージュ技法を加えた作品制作に取り組みはじめる。コラージュの素材には義兄が戦地から持ち帰った軍用毛布や蚊帳のほか、夫の三島茂司が所有する外国の新聞や雑誌、印刷会社が廃棄したポスターやチラシなどを選び、画面に貼りつけた。

最初期に制作された《Work 60-B》（1960年、no. 8）には2つの映画ポスター、アフリカ系アメリカ人歌手レイ・チャールズの映画『星空』（1965年）の梅田スカラ座上映を告知するもの、ジョン・リー・トンプソン監督の『死刑台への招待』（1965年）が用いられている。『死刑台への招待』は、ちょうど銃口の円が半分になるように割かれた状態で画面の左上と右下に貼られ、中央に貼られた群青色の三菱電機冷蔵庫の広告―水色の長方形を数珠繋ぎにした―を破り半円にしたものと呼応する配置となっている。円のモチーフはまた、画面右上にあるユニセフがノーベル平和賞に輝いたことを報じる『LIFE』の特集記事で、アフリカの子供たちが牛乳を飲む円形の食器にも見られる（1965年11月5日）。

三島のコラージュは、特定の図像を切り抜いてその組み合わせで新たなイメージを創造するのではなく、破いた紙片を貼り合わせて画面を構成する。《作品 65-H》（1965年、no. 11）では『LIFE』から3つの記事、教皇聖パウロ6世のアメリカ訪問（1965年10月15日）、写真家ジョン・ミリによる裸婦の連続写真（1966年12月23日）、リゾート地アカプルコでのファッションスナップ（1967年1月27日）が貼られている。

団体展やコンクール出展作品からも窺えるように、1960年代は印刷物をコラージュした油彩画に打ち込む時期となった。『毎日デイリーニューズ』などの新聞で画面を大胆に構成した《Work 64-III》（1964年、no. 10）では、紙片を帯状に貼った部分に東芝のテープレコーダーやフランスベッドの広告が確認できる。なかでも、一際目を惹くのは銘菓「神戸風月堂」が1957年に考案した包装紙で、赤地の上には白抜きの店名ロゴと黒色の商品名と神戸のランドマークが散りばめられており、油彩で台形に黒く塗られた部分とあわせて本作のアクセントとなっている。それは《Work-64-I》（1964年、no. 9）でも同様に、画面右下に貼られたコーヒー会社の懸賞記事と食前酒「デュボネ」のロゴの赤色が画面にリズムを与えている。また本作品では航空にかかわる記事が使用されており、紺と黒の油彩で記事を囲むように塗った画面上部は、旅客機の窓を連想させる。

ラジオから流れる音楽をBGMに夜中まで制作する三島を象徴するように、《変貌 III》（1966年、no. 12）は音楽への興味関心が溢れた作品である。ジャズ・フルート奏者ハービー・マンの紹介記事や指揮者ルドルフ・バルシャイの公演案内のほか、フィデラ社のステレオデッキやビクター社のレコードプレイヤーの広告といった音楽再生機器の図版が散見される。また上から薄く青を塗った部分があるほか、青系統の印刷物として「Jazz Vocal Series」の広告や『LIFE』のワッツ暴動にまつわる記事（1966年7月15日）、ジュール・ヴェルヌ原作の映画『海底二万哩』（1954年）のポスターなどが用いられている。そして画面上部には、1966年に来日したピアニストのアルトゥー

図1　三島喜美代《ヴィーナスの変貌II》1966年　新聞紙、雑誌、シルクスクリーン、合板

ル・ルービンシュタインにかんする記事の同じ箇所が8枚貼られている。黒い紙に2段で組まれた本記事は並べて貼ることで模様のような効果を生む。この連貼りによる図像の反復は、シルクスクリーンの作品へと繋がっていく。

1966年頃から、三島はシルクスクリーンを用いたシリーズ作品「ヴィーナスの変貌」を制作する。本シリーズはサンドロ・ボッティチェリの傑作のひとつ《ヴィーナスの誕生》(1482-85年頃)に描かれた愛と美の女神を種々に転写するというもので、《ヴィーナスの変貌II》(1966年、[図1])では、画面上部に薬の広告を11枚連貼りするという従来のコラージュも行いつつ、左右を反転させた4体のヴィーナスのシルエットを少しずつ重なるように横に並べる。

《ヴィーナスの変貌V》(1967年、no. 14)では、ネガとポジに反転させた36体の女神を画面の上下左右に白、黒、水色で転写する。中央の黒い矩形に転写された6体のうち白色の1体は、右側の黒色のシルエットと対をなす。他方、『LIFE』の記事で複数枚コラージュした上に25体の女神を転写した《ヴィーナスの変貌VI》(1967年)は、記事も女神も認識しづらい「イメージの氾濫」といった画面になっている。

シルクスクリーンの次なる連作といえる「女優」シリーズでは、《Untitled》(1970年、no. 17)や《Untitled》(1970-71年、no. 18)においてネガに反転させた女たちで画面全体を覆い尽くす。女たちの図像は、歌手で俳優のバーブラ・ストレイサンドを特集する『LIFE』からの一枚である。「シャネル」のショーを見学するバーブラ、映画俳優のマレーネ・ディートリヒとエルザ・マルティネリの3名を撮らえたもので、三島はこの写真をいくつかの作品に取り入れている。《[題名不詳]》(1971年、[図2])では、左端に座るバーブラを削除する代わりにディートリヒが腰を下ろす椅子の足を描き足す。一方、これに近しい構図で白、黒、赤色を基調とする《題名不詳》(1971年)では、右端のマルティネリを転写で2人に増やすといった実験を試みている。

「ヴィーナスの変貌」や「女優」シリーズの制作と時を同じくして、三島は陶に新聞を転写した立体作品の制作を開始する。以後、コミック・ブックや段ボールなど様々に展開するが、シルクスクリーンの技法がこれら作品の誕生を技術的な面で支えたことは言うまでもない。コラージュとシルクスクリーンに選ばれた印刷物からは、三島がその時代に感じた「現代」が記録されている。

(練馬区立美術館 学芸員)

図2　三島喜美代《[題名不詳]》1971年　新聞、油彩、シルクスクリーン、カンヴァス　東京都現代美術館所蔵

Mishima Kimiyo and Printed Matter of the 1960s and Early 1970s: Selection of Imagery for Collages and Silkscreens

Arai Hikaru

In the early 1960s, Mishima Kimiyo began incorporating collage into her oil paintings. The materials she affixed to her canvases included military blankets and mosquito nets that her brother-in-law had brought back from the battlefield, foreign newspapers and magazines collected by her husband Mishima Shigeji, and posters and flyers discarded by printing companies.

One of her earliest pieces, *Work 60-B* (1960, no. 8), utilizes two movie posters. One promotes the screening, at the Umeda Scala Theater in Osaka, of Ray Charles's film *Ballad in Blue* (1965), and the other advertises director John Lee Thompson's *Return from The Ashes* (1965). The *Return from The Ashes* poster is positioned in such a way that the mouth of a gun barrel is split in half, one half appearing at the top left and the other at the bottom right of the canvas. This arrangement complements a torn and halved circular motif from an ultramarine blue advertisement for a Mitsubishi electric refrigerator, which features a sequence of light-blue rectangles. The circle is further echoed in a feature article from *Life* magazine, positioned in the top right of the canvas, which reports on UNICEF's winning the Nobel Peace Prize, with more circles visible in the round dishes from which African children drink milk (November 5, 1965).

In her collages, Mishima did not create new images by neatly cutting out and combining pictures. Instead, she constructed compositions by piecing together torn fragments of printed matter. In *Work 65-H* (1965, no. 11), she attached three articles from *Life*, covering Pope Paul VI's visit to the US (October 15, 1965), a sequence of nude photographs by Gjon Mili (December 23, 1966) , and fashion snapshots from the Mexican resort of Acapulco (January 27, 1967).

During the 1960s, Mishima devoted herself to oil painting enhanced with collaged printed matter, as is evident from her contributions to group exhibitions and competitions. In *Work 64-III* (1964, no. 10), she made bold use of newspapers such as the *Mainichi Daily News*, covering parts of the canvas with strips of paper bearing ads for Toshiba tape recorders and beds by France Bed. Her use of wrapping paper designed in 1957 for the renowned confectioner Kobe Fugetsudo, with a red background, white store logo, black products name, and scattered images of Kobe landmarks, is particularly striking. These elements resonate with a trapezoidal area of black oil paint, and serve as focal points of the composition. A similar approach is used in *Work-64-I* (1964, no. 9), in which an article on a coffee company contest affixed to the lower right corner of the canvas and the red logo of the aperitif liqueur Dubonnet impart rhythm to the picture. The work also incorporates an article on aviation, and the upper part of the canvas, with navy blue and black oil paint surrounding the article, evokes the windows of a passenger plane.

As if reflecting Mishima's practice of working late into the night with music from the radio in the background, *Transfiguration III* (1966, no. 12) brims with passion for music. The work features various music-related elements such as an article on jazz flutist Herbie Mann, an announcement of a concert conducted by Rudolf Barshai, and ads for audio equipment such as Fidela stereo tape decks and Victor record players. It includes sections lightly brushed over in blue, and incorporates blue printed matter in the form of ads for the Jazz Vocal Series, a *Life* article about the Watts uprising in Los Angeles (July 15, 1966), and a poster for the 1954 movie *20,000 Leagues Under the Sea* based on Jules Verne's novel. At the top of the canvas, the same pages of an article about pianist Arthur Rubinstein's 1966 visit to Japan is repeated eight times, and the article's two paragraphs printed on black paper produce a rhythmic pattern effect. This approach to image repetition anticipates Mishima's later adoption of silkscreen.

Around 1966, Mishima began a series of silkscreen works titled *Transfiguration of Venus*, which presents various reinterpretations of the goddess of love and beauty as depicted in Botticelli's master piece *The Birth of Venus* (c. 1482-85). *Transfiguration of Venus II* (1966, p. 77 top) employs Mishima's existing collage approach with a row of eleven medicine advertisements at the top, but also arrays four silhouettes of Venus, flipped left to right and arrayed horizontally across the picture so that each slightly overlaps the next.

In *Transfiguration of Venus V* (1967, no. 14), 36 images of the goddess, positive-negative reversed, are printed in white, black, and light blue around the edges of the picture. In a black rectangle in the center are six images of Venus, one of which, in white, forms a pair with a black silhouette on the right side. Meanwhile, *Transfiguration of Venus VI* (1967) presents a "flood of images," with 25 Venus images superimposed on a collage of multiple articles from *Life*, rendering both the articles and the goddesses virtually indecipherable.

Mishima's subsequent silkscreen series, *Actress*, includes *Untitled* (1970, no. 17) and *Untitled* (1970-71, no. 18), which fill the pictorial space entirely with negative-positive reversed images of women. These images are derived from a *Life* magazine feature on singer and actress Barbra Streisand (March 18, 1966), with a photo of her at a Chanel fashion show with fellow actresses Marlene Dietrich and Elsa Martinelli. Mishima incorporated this photograph into multiple works. One work from 1971 (title unknown, p. 77 bottom) omits Streisand, who is seated on the left, and puts the leg of Dietrich's chair in her place. Another work (title unknown), featuring a composition similar to the aforementioned works and a white, black, and red color scheme, experiments by duplicating Martinelli's figure on the right edge through image transfer.

Concurrently with the *Transfiguration of Venus* and *Actress* series, Mishima began producing three-dimensional works by silkscreening newspaper images onto ceramics. She subsequently extended this technique to encompass comic books, cardboard boxes and more. It is clear that silkscreen printing was technically crucial to the realization of these works. Mishima's selection of printed matter for her collages and silkscreens serves as a record of "the present day" as she experienced it at the time.

(Curator, Nerima Art Museum)

2

割れる印刷物 1970年頃～

Breakable Printed Matter: Circa 1970 Onward

第2章　割れる印刷物　1970年頃〜

土を紙のように薄く伸ばし、シルクスクリーンや手書きによって陶土の表面に新聞やチラシの文字を転写して焼成する―この技法によって三島は立体作品「割れる印刷物」を生み出し、半世紀にわたり独自の表現として展開してきた。紙に印刷された情報を陶に写し替える自らの制作行為を、三島は「情報の化石化」と呼ぶ。硬く、安定しているかに見えながら、扱いによっては脆く、割れやすい陶は、三島にとっては、日々大量に作られては捨てられていく印刷物と組み合わせることによって、不安感や恐怖感を表現するのにうってつけの素材となった。

割れる印刷物は、新聞やチラシ、コミックから始まり、段ボール、フィルム、紙袋、封筒、飲料ボトルなど身の回りの様々な日用品に及んだ。それらの多くは実物大に近く、一見すると本物と見紛うほどで、遊び心やユーモアを感じさせるが、三島の主眼はスーパーリアリズム風のだまし絵的オブジェを作ることではない。日常生活にあるものを異化作用を通して、情報洪水の危機や不安を顕在化させ、再認識させるところに三島の挑戦があった。

1980年代以降、三島は作品を巨大化して、見る者の視点にさらに揺さぶりをかける。陶による異化作用を経てもなお、紙の薄さや質感はそのままに緊張感をはらんでいた新聞紙の作品は、頑丈なマッスによるモニュメンタルな彫刻へと変貌した（nos. 47, 48）。また、剥げかかったビラまで再現したコンクリートの電柱を模した作品、新作発表の場となった画廊の柱を模した作品（no. 49）など、技術的には難しいとされていた陶の巨大化を成功させ、ポップ・アート的な明るさや楽しさを発揮した。作品の巨大化は、この後壮大なスケールによるインスタレーションやパブリックアートというかたちをとって、三島の代表作へとつながっていく。

2. Breakable Printed Matter: Circa 1970 Onward

By flattening clay to paper-like thinness and silkscreening or hand-painting text from newspapers and flyers onto its surface before firing, Mishima created the distinctive three-dimensional "breakable printed matter." For half a century, this artistic practice, which Mishima describes as "the fossilization of information," has been her signature mode of expression. Despite the apparent hardness and stability of ceramics, their inherent fragility and tendency to break when not handled with care made them an ideal medium for Mishima to articulate anxiety and dread when thematically combined with relentlessly mass-produced and discarded printed matter.

The "breakable printed matter" series began with newspapers, flyers, and comics, and has since expanded to include a vast array of everyday objects including cardboard boxes, film, paper bags, envelopes, and beverage bottles. These works, often life-sized, can easily be mistaken for the real thing at a glance, giving them an element of playfulness and humor. However, Mishima's main intent was not to craft super-realist objects that deceive the eye. Rather, she sought to manifest a sense of crisis and unease arising from information overload, strategically transforming mundane items so that we see them in a new light.

In the 1980s Mishima began creating larger works that more radically disrupted viewers' perspectives. Earlier works with newspaper had preserved the innate tension of newspaper's thinness and texture despite being transformed into ceramic. However, later works with the same motif were shaped into sturdy forms and turned into monumental sculptures (nos. 47, 48). She has also succeeded in enlarging ceramic creations that were technically challenging to scale up, producing works that replicate concrete utility poles adorned with peeling posters, or the columns of a gallery where she showed her new works (no. 49), delivering Pop Art-inflected vibrancy and humor. This escalation in scale paved the way for large-scale installations and public art projects that are among Mishima's most iconic works.

20-1　Paper Bag E-1　1973年

20-2　Paper Bag E-5　1973年

20-3　Paper Bag E-6　1974年

20-4　Paper Bag E-S1　1977年

20-5　Paper Bag E-S2　1977年

20-6　Paper Bag E-S3　1977年

20-7　Paper Bag E-S4　1977年

20-8　Paper Bag E-7　1980年

兵庫陶芸美術館

20-1

20-7

20-5

20-8

22
Package '74
1973-74年
滋賀県立陶芸の森 陶芸館

Industry
Masters

23～29
Untitled
1975年

23

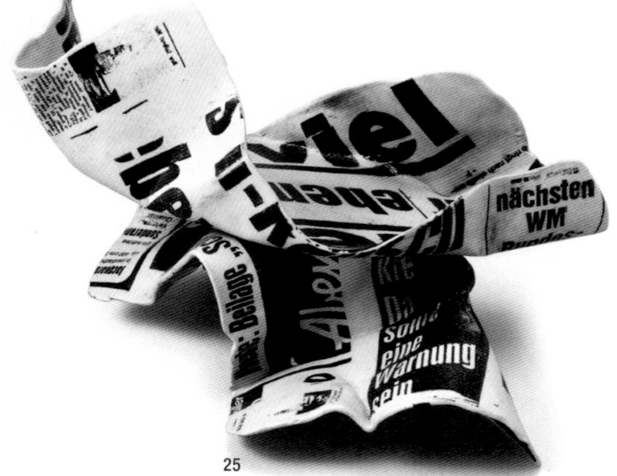

25

24

26

27

28

29

30
Film 75
1975年

30

31, 32
Newspaper 76
1976年

31

32

39
Notebook 80
1980年

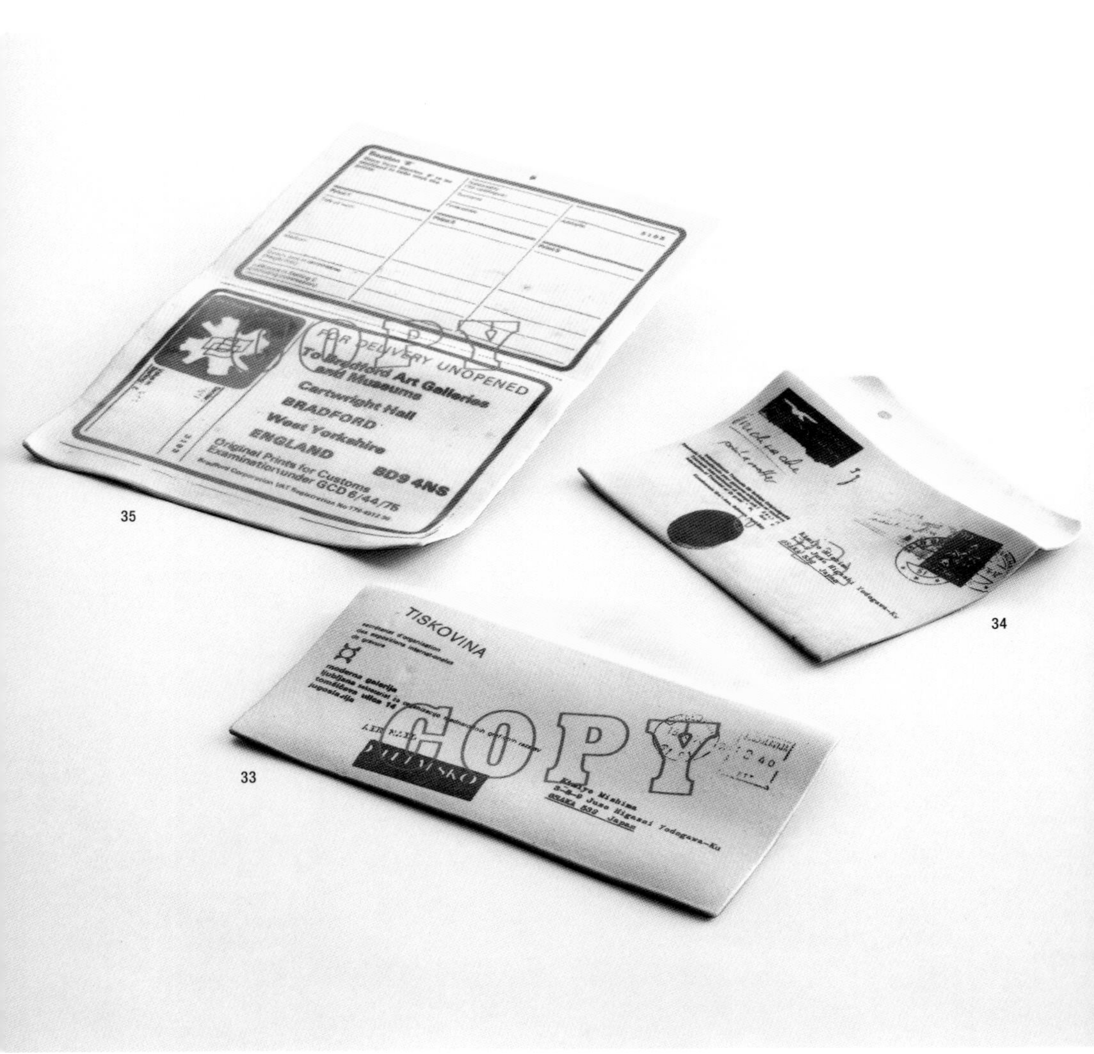

33, 34
Copy 76
1976年

35
Copy 78
1978年

21
D-1
1973年

36

37

36
球 Copy-78-A4
Ball: Copy-78-A4
1978年

37
球 Copy-78-A5
Ball: Copy-78-A5
1978年

38
Package '78
1978年
滋賀県立陶芸の森 陶芸館

日本向け特選
PRECOOLED BEEORE LOADING FOR YOUR PROTECTION
CAL FAME
CALIFORNIA
LEMONS
日本向け特選
CAL FAME
CALIFORNIA
LEMONS
MZ-10

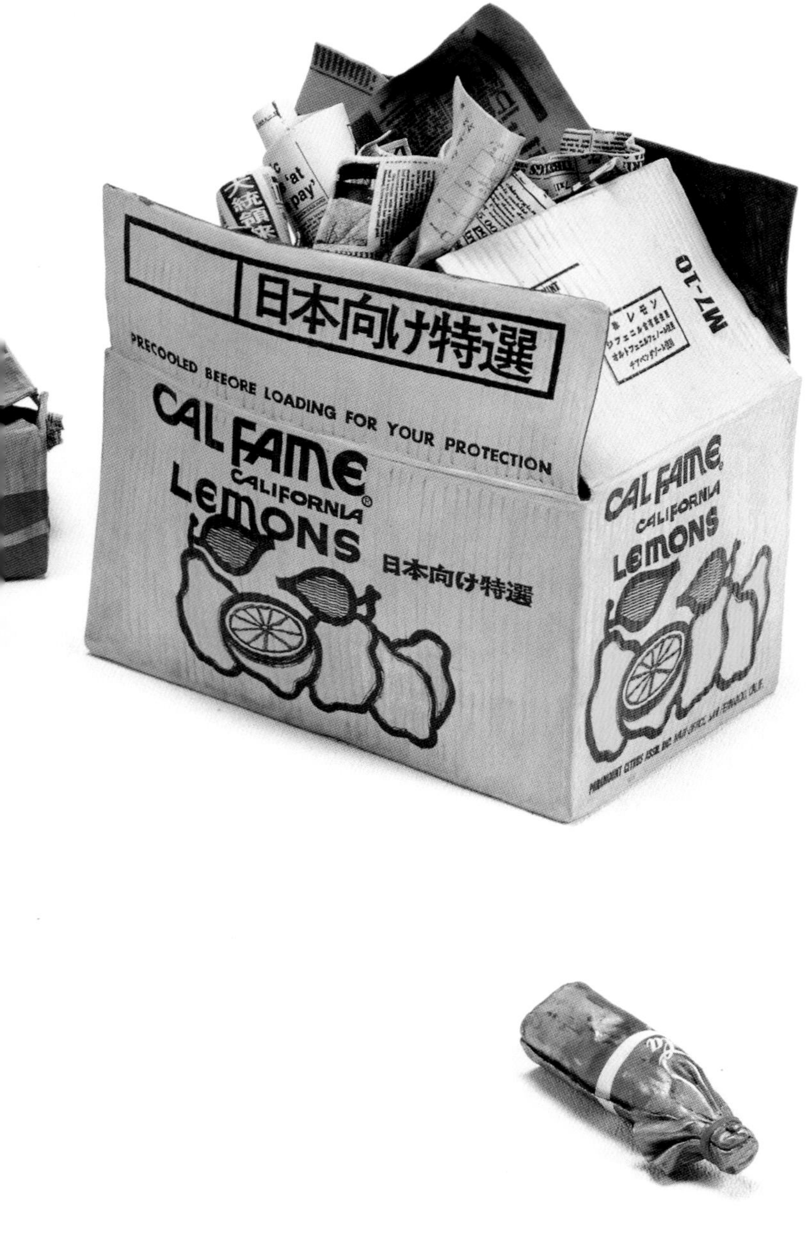

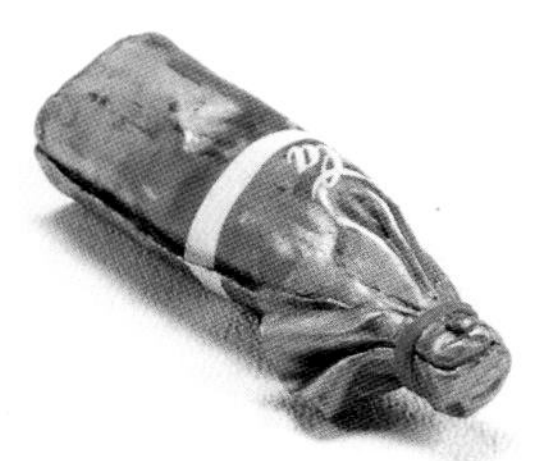

40
Comic Book '80
1980年
滋賀県立陶芸の森 陶芸館

北の球児
なんと孫六
村生ミオ登場!
STAR WARS
森永
スターウォーズ
キャラメル

41, 45
Untitled
1981年

45

青幻舎
SEIGENSHA ART PUBLISHING

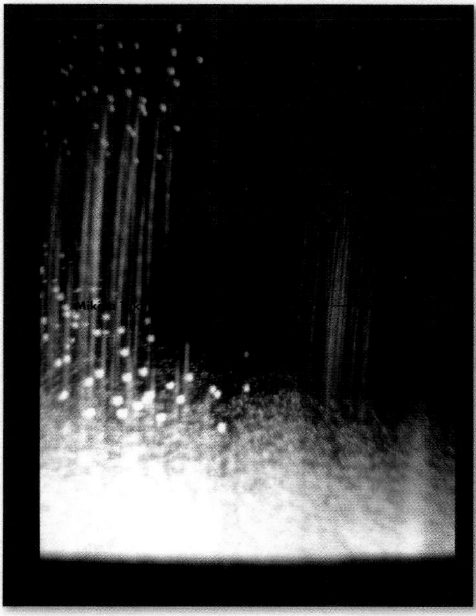

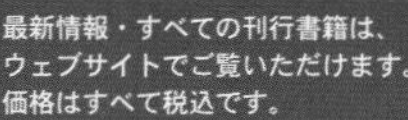
最新情報・すべての刊行書籍は、
ウェブサイトでご覧いただけます。
価格はすべて税込です。

MAGNUM MAGNUM
増補改訂版

編集：ブリジット・ラルディノワ

20世紀の偉人から近代の巨匠、現代の新星まで、写真家のビジョンや想像力、才能を讃え、最高のマグナム・フォトを紹介する一冊。

**A4変型／ 728 頁／上製本（布張り）
定価：22,000 円**

私のためのポートレイト

著：小野啓

写真家 小野啓が 2002 年から続けてきた日本全国の高校生を被写体としたポートレートシリーズの集大成。

B5変型／ 128 頁／上製本／定価：4,400 円

まだ見ぬソール・ライター
THE UNSEEN SAUL LEITER

著：ソール・ライター ほか

アトリエに遺された約 1 万点の未公開スライドから厳選された 76 点を収録。ソール・ライターの美意識の真骨頂、"ストリート・フォト"の決定版。

A4変型／ 160 頁／上製本／定価 4,180 円

ソール・ライター
Saul Leiter The Centennial Retrospective

著：ソール・ライター ほか

膨大なアーカイブをもとにソール・ライターの全貌に迫る。生誕100年を記念した特別版、世界 8 カ国で刊行！

**310×260mm ／ 352 頁／上製本
定価：9,680 円**

44

48

47, 48
Untitled
1984年

12jährig
Wies
Mode
Heute: Beilage
B 1017 A
18.50
Rotes Kreuz
Wies'n
TOP
MÖBEL-MARKT
AZ München
12jähriger nach
Wies'n-Raus
macht Mode
en lassen
Münchner
Schön
bleibt
bis zur
nächsten
zur Wies'n
bis 1978 verlängert

47

46
Newspaper 83
1983年

51

50

Ecofin, Paris ve
er la feuille de rou
G20 d'avril
résident du groupe
nat. Pour l'instant,
Orange
Dow Jones
CAC 40
X-Dax
La cote
Les marchés

本日限り!
7月23日(日)
Cola
TEL (302)

52
Untitled
1990年

53
FOCUS 91
1991年

57
楽譜
Musical Score
2007年
岐阜県現代陶芸美術館

53

57

54
WORK C-92
1991-92年
岐阜県現代陶芸美術館

ILEX
Fresh
PINEAPPLE
DISTRIBUTED WORLDWIDE BY
DEL MONTE TROPICAL FRUIT COMPANY
Fresh
BANANAS
Fresh BANANAS
LEMONS

55
サンキスボックス
Sunkis Box
2005年
岐阜県現代陶芸美術館

Quest
Talks on Federal Takeov
Medicaid Stopped — U
to Keep Food Stamps
30778
L-10/02
OF THE FOLLOWING:

PREMIUM BANANAS
PREMIUM
Chiquita
PALLETIZED
PS
PREMIUM BANANAS
DISTRIBUTED BY:
CHIQUITA UNIFRUTTI ASIA
PREMIUM
Chiquita
PALLETIZED
PS

56
バナナボックス
Banana Box
2007年
岐阜県現代陶芸美術館

65
Box Orange 19
2019年

67
Work 22-Sunkist 2
2022年

58-1
リーフレット(赤)
Leaflet [Red]
2007-08年
岐阜県現代陶芸美術館

58-2
リーフレット(青)
Leaflet [Blue]
2007-08年
岐阜県現代陶芸美術館

不況を揺がす大型企画!!
特別
大廉売!
5月31日
OPEN
全商品オール
2割引ヨリ
5割引マデ
TEL(302)-7316番
オール商品
赤札付き
5割〜7割引

63

62

59

59～64
KOUKOKU 08
2008年

61

60

64

Work 20-T
2020年

68
Work 23-TAG
2023年

3

ゴミと向き合う

Grappling with Garbage

第3章　ゴミと向き合う

三島が印刷物を作品制作に使い始めた時期は、電子メディアが今ほどには決定的に普及していなかった時代であり、情報が膨大であればあるほど、物理的なゴミの量も膨大になる現実があった。当初は情報に埋没する不安感や危機感を表現していた三島であったが、次第にその問題意識は、情報からゴミへと移って行った。否、ゴミへと戻って行ったという言い方の方が正確かもしれない。もともと、三島がコラージュや陶によるオブジェで使っていた新聞や雑誌、チラシは、彼女の身近にあって日常生活の中で消費された後の情報のゴミにほかならず、ゴミを使って作品を制作するというスタイル自体は終始一貫しているのである。

空き缶や段ボールなど身近なゴミを題材に陶で再現した作品に加え、1990年前後から、三島作品に使われる素材も多様化している。環境への意識を高めていた三島は、制作に欠かせない陶土も有限の資源であると聞くと、再生素材である溶融スラグ（産業廃棄物を1,400度で焼成して生成されるガラス状の粉末）と廃土を混ぜた土を使って制作を行なうようになる（nos. 73-75）。さらに近年は、自ら収集したブリキ缶、鉄くず、廃車のパーツなど廃材そのものも作品に取り込んでいる（no. 81）。本人は事あるごとに「ゴミからゴミを作る」と発言しているが、こうした廃材から成る作品にも印刷物の文字は登場し、三島作品としての一貫性は維持されている。

ゴミに象徴される環境問題は21世紀の世界に深刻な陰を落としているが、三島の作品はシリアスな批評をはらみつつも、エコロジー的な考えを声高に叫ぶものとはなっていない。「ゴミはその土地の残骸みたいなもので、暮らしぶりが表れる。そして作品は私の考え、生活から出たもの」*と三島は言い、ゴミを社会の現実の反映ととらえ、そこに眼差しを向けてひたすら作品を作り続けている。「自身の作品を通してゴミ問題をユーモアをもって感じてもらえたら」と三島は願うのである。

＊「現代美術家 80才代で脚光」読売新聞、2023年3月2日夕刊

3. Grappling with Garbage

In the era when Mishima began working with printed matter, the world was not yet dominated by electronic media, and an increasing volume of information visibly resulted in more physical waste. Initially, Mishima's work conveyed anxiety and a sense of crisis resulting from being deluged by information, but over time, her focus shifted from information toward garbage itself. Perhaps it would be more accurate to say her focus "returned" to garbage. The newspapers, magazines, and flyers embedded in her collages and ceramic works were tangible byproducts of the information in her surroundings, consumed in the course of daily life, reflecting a consistent career-long concern with transforming garbage into art.

In addition to reproducing everyday garbage like empty cans and cardboard boxes in ceramic, Mishima diversified the materials in her works from around 1990, driven by heightened awareness of environmental concerns. Upon recognizing that the clay she relied on was a finite resource, she began incorporating molten slag (a glass-like material created by melting down waste at high temperatures) and discarded clay mixtures into her works (nos. 73-75). In more recent years, she has also included scavenged items such as tin cans, scrap iron, and scrapped car parts into her art (no. 81). She has frequently spoken of "making garbage out of garbage," but her works continue to feature printed text, maintaining thematic consistency throughout her oeuvre.

Amid the grave environmental challenges of the 21st century, Mishima's art presents a serious, critical, yet not overbearing perspective on ecological issues. She views garbage as a mirror reflecting our lifestyles and values, stating: "Garbage is like the wreckage of our civilization, revealing our way of life. And my works are also manifestations of my thinking and my everyday life."* Mishima hopes to "engage people with the problem of garbage through [her] art, to deliver insights with a sense of humor."

* "Gendai bijutsuka 80 dai de kyakko" [Contemporary Artist Earning High Acclaim in Her 80s], *Yomiuri Shimbun*, evening edition, March 2, 2023.

70
Work 90-BG
1990年

69
Work 86-B
1987年

72

71

78

72
Work 92-N2
1992年

71
Work 92-N1
1992年

78
Work 21-B
2021年

73
Comic Book 03-1
2003年
ポーラ美術館

74
Comic Book 03-2
2003年
ポーラ美術館

73

75
Comic Book 03-3
2003年

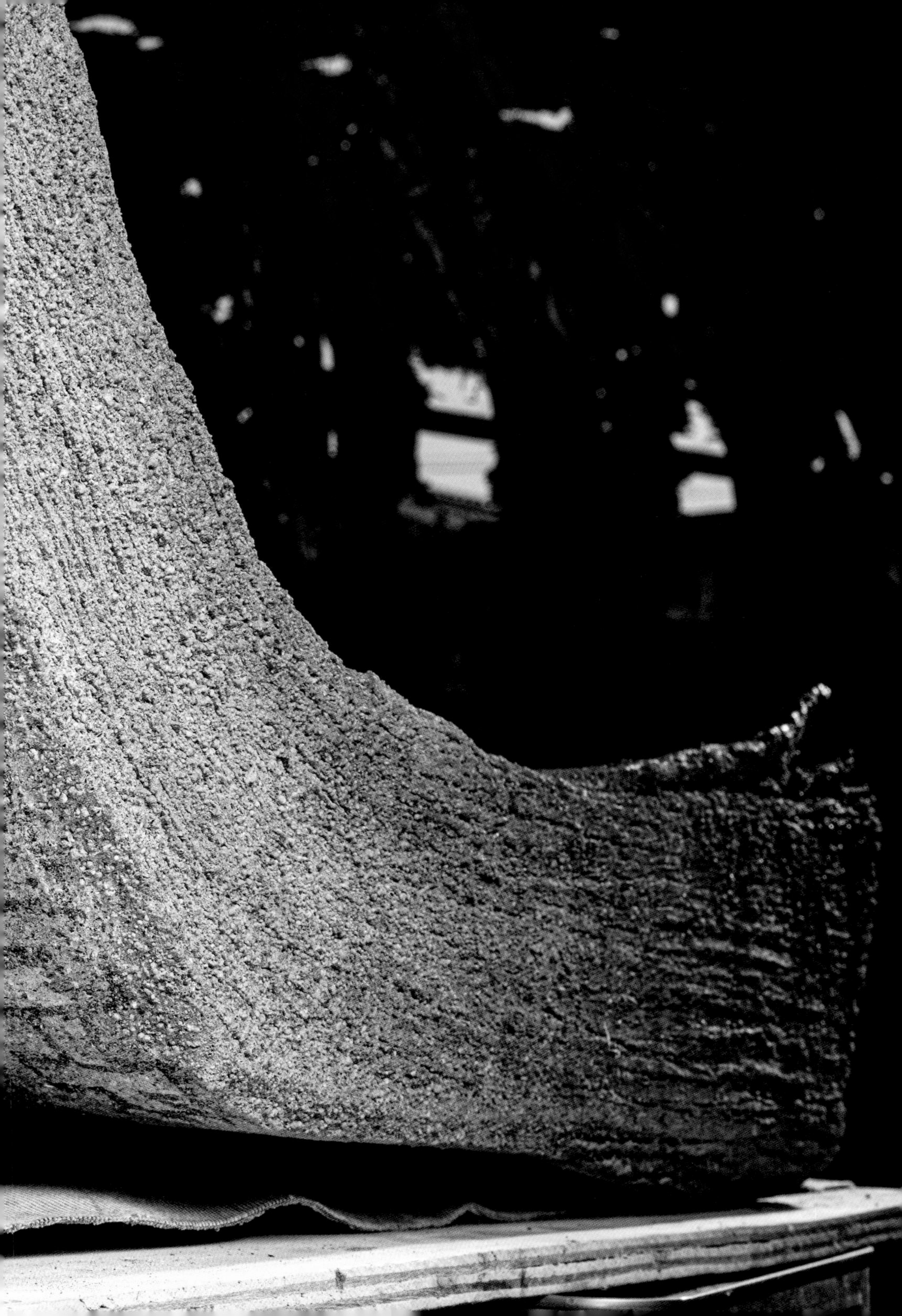

AND TASTY
ORIGINAL BREW

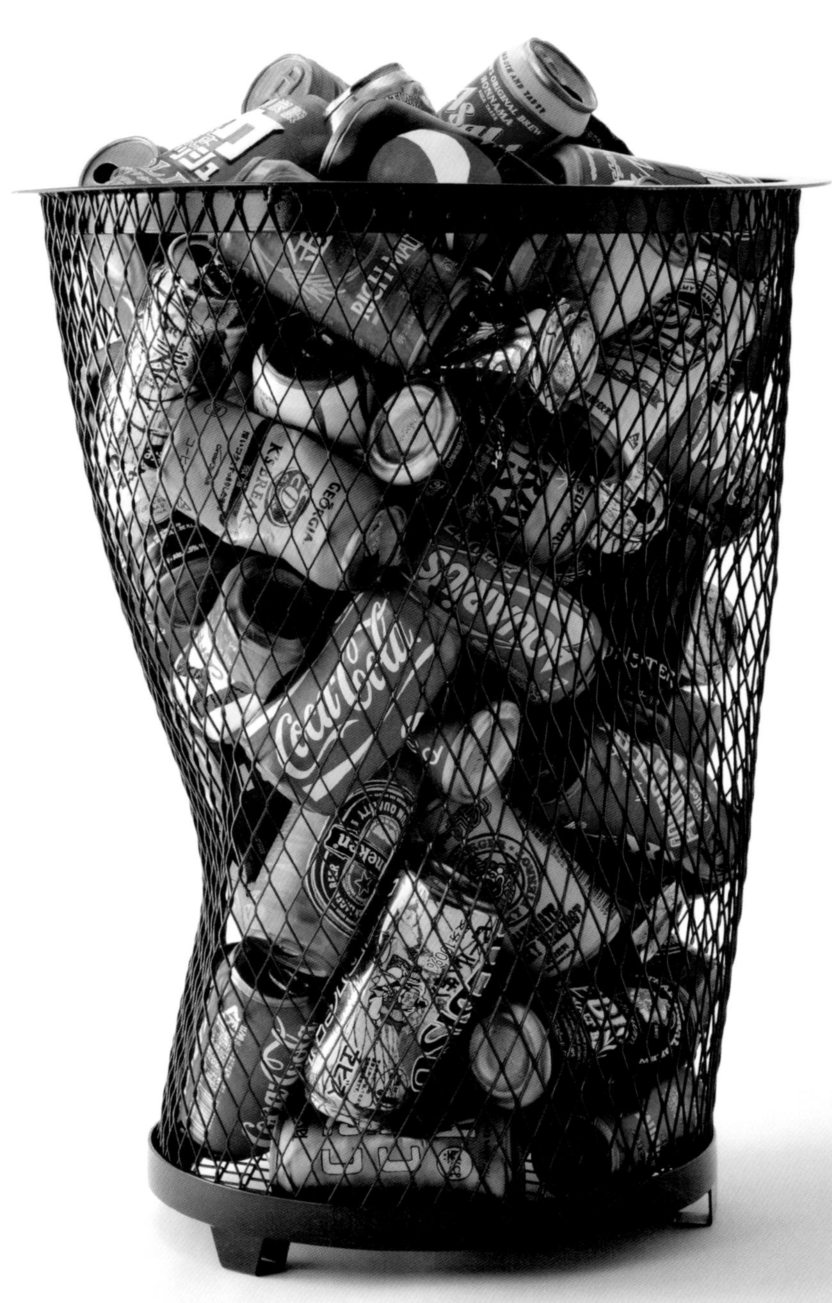

77
Work 17-C
2017年
ポーラ美術館

79

79
Work 21-G
2021年

80
Work 21-C2
2021年

POCARI SWEAT
ION SUPPLY DRINK
CA
KK-114
Coca-Cola light

81
Work 22-P
2022年

Mobil

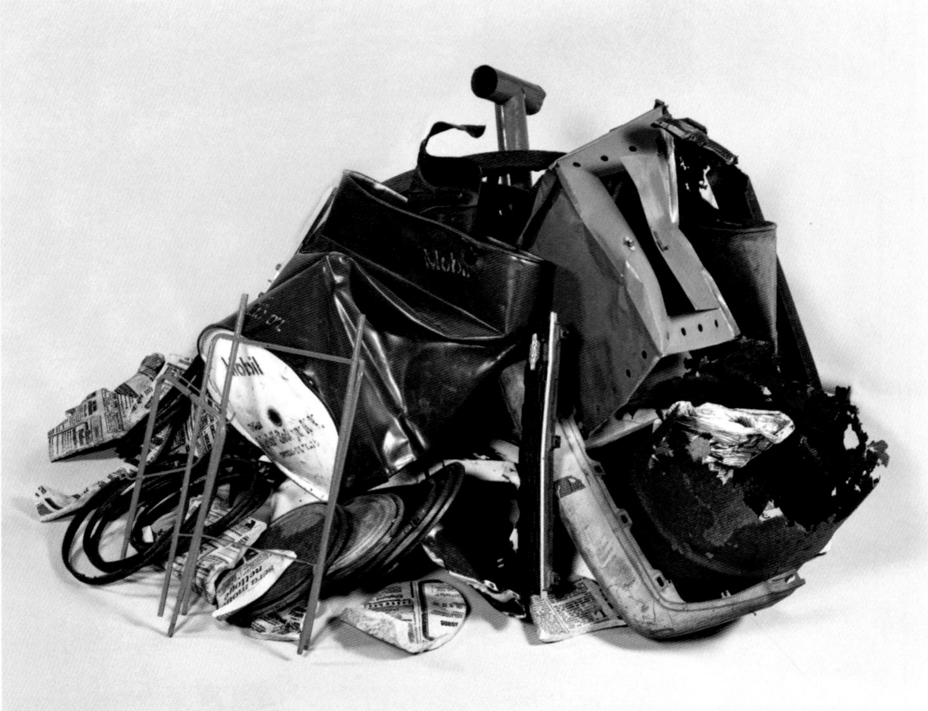

76
Work 17-POT
2017年

4

大型インスタレーション

Large-Scale Installations

第4章　大型インスタレーション

作品の巨大化は、1980年代中頃に始まる大規模なインスタレーションによって頂点に達した。その代表作《20世紀の記憶》(no. 82) は、約200平方メートルの床一面に、使い古した耐火レンガ・ブロック1万個余りをぎっしり敷き詰めている。各レンガの表面には三島が20世紀の100年間から抜き出した新聞記事が転写され、文字通り20世紀の記憶の断片が視覚化されるとともに、その時代に向き合った彼女自身の記憶が刻まれているように思われる。不揃いのレンガによって眼前に広がる沈黙の風景は、時が凍結したかのようであり、SFチックな情報洪水の成れの果てのようにも、戦争によって焼け野原になってしまった都市の廃墟のようにも見える。ともあれ、先行きが不透明な現代という時代にあって、三島が刻印した20世紀の記憶を、来るべき未来への記憶として改めて受け止めていただきたい。

もう一つの大型インスタレーションに、陶製の新聞や雑誌を高さ2メートルを越える直方体上に積み上げた作品《Work 92-N》(p.168, fig. 6) がある。三島が旅先から持ち帰った印刷物なども含めて束ねたこの作品では、情報の物質的側面が強調されている。どんな情報も読み終わった途端即全部ゴミになるという三島の言葉のとおり、情報洪水はゴミの問題へと帰結することが圧倒的な物量をもって示されている。ちなみに上述の2作品は、ともに普段は東京のART FACTORY城南島に常設展示されている。

作品の巨大化は、各地に設置されたパブリックアート作品にも見ることができる。産業廃棄物がかつて不法投棄された香川県直島では、島の再生を願い、三島は高さ4.5mの巨大なごみ箱を模した作品を現地に恒久設置した。本展に出品の3つのごみ箱作品 (nos. 77, 79-80) は、これに連なるもので、カラフルな陶の空き缶や段ボールの断片が金網のごみ箱に放り込まれている。本物と区別できないほどのリアルさに、思わず微笑んでしまう人も多いだろう。《20世紀の記憶》が掻き立てる不穏さと、ごみ箱作品が見せる日常性やユーモアとのギャップの大きさには戸惑わされるが、ともに三島が長い時間をかけて追い求めてきた世界が集約されている。

4. Large-Scale Installations

The enlargement of Mishima's works culminated after mid-1980s with her venture into monumentally sized installations. In a seminal work, *Memories of the 20th Century* (no. 82), she covered an entire floor some 200 square meters in size with over 10,000 densely laid reclaimed fire-retardant brick blocks. These are imprinted with newspaper articles that Mishima selected from throughout the 20th century, literally rendering visible a hundred years of fragmented memories while seemingly engraving them with her own memories of those times. The array of uneven bricks becomes a silent, expansive landscape, evoking images of a science-fictional world frozen in time by an overwhelming flood of information, or the desolation of a war-ravaged city. In any case, this work allows the viewer to re-engage with memories of the 20th century embedded by Mishima, and may offer some insight for the future amid the uncertainty of our current era.

In another large-scale installation, *Work 92-N* (p.168, fig. 6), she assembled ceramic renditions of newspapers and magazines into a towering rectangular structure over two meters in height. Composed of printed matter, including items collected by Mishima during her travels, the work emphasizes the tangible aspect of information. Echoing Mishima's observation that all information becomes garbage once consumed, the massive volume of the work vividly illustrates the direct link between information saturation and garbage overload. Both of these installations are usually on permanent view at Art Factory Jonanjima in Tokyo.

Mishima's shift to larger-scale works is also reflected in her public art projects at various sites. On Naoshima, an island in Kagawa Prefecture previously marred by illegal dumping of industrial waste, she installed a monumental 4.5-meter-tall trash can sculpture symbolizing her hopes for the island's revival. The trash can sculptures (nos. 77, 79-80) featured in this exhibition are related works. These wire-mesh trash cans brimming with vivid ceramic replicas of empty beverage cans and pieces of cardboard are so indistinguishable from the real thing that they will no doubt elicit smiles from viewers. The menace invoked by *Memories of the 20th Century* starkly contrasts with the familiarity and humor of the trash can sculptures, yet they both encapsulate the world that Mishima has explored over the course of her long career.

82
20世紀の記憶
Memories of the 20th Century
1984-2013年

83
化石になった情報 88
Fossilized Information 88
1986-88年

参考　大型インスタレーションおよびパブリックアート
Reference Exhibits: Large-Scale Installations and Public Art

fig. 1
Newspaper-84-E
1984年
陶、転写
105.0×74.0×102.0cm
原美術館 ARC

Newspaper-84-E
1984
Silkscreen on ceramic
105.0×74.0×102.0cm
Hara Museum ARC

fig. 2
Newspaper 84-W
1984年
陶、転写
135.0×110.0×105.0cm
太陽の森 ディマシオ美術館

Newspaper 84-W
1984
Silkscreen on ceramic
135.0×110.0×105.0cm
Di-Maccio Art Museum, The Forest of Taiyo

fig. 3
Package-88-T
1988年
陶、転写
300.0×123.0×146.0cm
岐阜県土岐市(東濃中部医療センター土岐市立総合病院)

Package-88-T
1988
Silkscreen on ceramic
300.0×123.0×146.0cm
Toki City, Gifu Prefecture(Tono Chubu Hospital Center, Toki Municipal General Hospital)

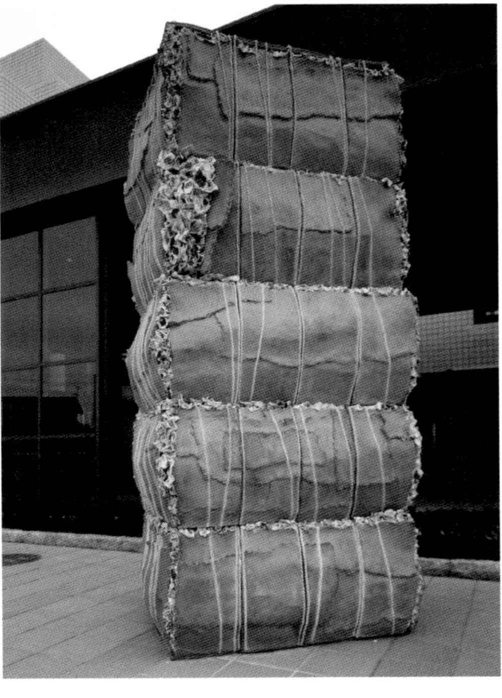

fig. 4
固められた情報90
1990年
陶、転写、火山灰、FRP、鉄、木
各53.0×110.0×110.0cm(16個)
個人蔵(ART FACTORY城南島)

Wreck of Time 90
1990
Silkscreen on ceramic,
volcanic ashes, FRP, iron, wood
each 53.0×110.0×110.0cm
(16 pieces)
Private Collection
(ART FACTORY Jonanjima)

fig. 6
Work 92-N
1990-92年
陶、転写
227.0×390.0×490.0cm
個人蔵（ART FACTORY 城南島）

Work 92-N
1990-92
Silkscreen on ceramic
227.0×390.0×490.0cm
Private Collection (ART FACTORY Jonanjima)

fig. 5
Newspaper P-91
1990-91年
陶、転写、銅、鉄、セメント
166.5×126.0×90.0cm
大原美術館

Newspaper P-91
1990-91
Silkscreen on ceramic, bronze, iron, cement
166.5×126.0×90.0cm
Ohara Museum of Art

fig. 7
Newspaper 08
1997-2008年
ポリエステル、転写
300.0×1500.0×1000.0cm
個人蔵（ART FACTORY 城南島）

Newspaper 08
1997-2008
Silkscreen on polyester
300.0×1500.0×1000.0cm
Private Collection (ART FACTORY Jonanjima)

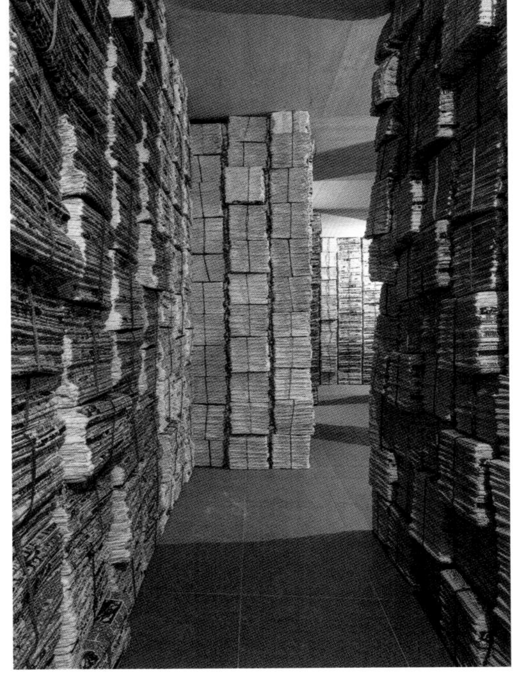

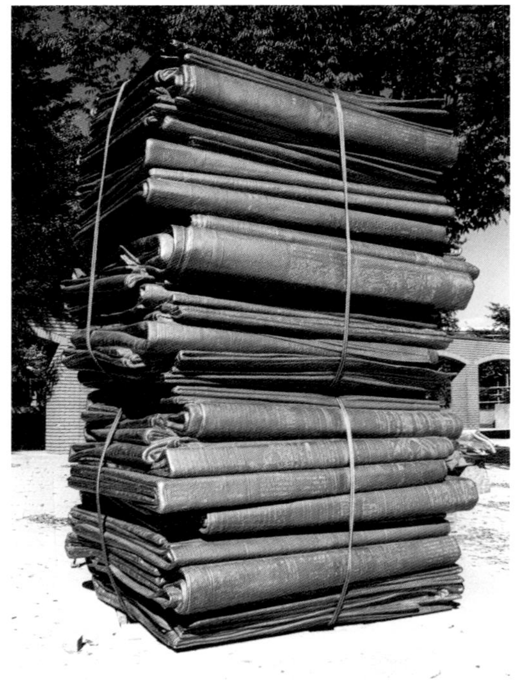

fig. 8
Newspaper 97-A
1997年
アルミニウム合金、ステンレス鋼線材
320.0×200.0×180.0cm
埼玉県桶川市（桶川駅西口公園）

Newspaper 97-A
1997
Aluminum alloy, stainless steel
320.0×200.0×180.0cm
Saitama Prefecture Okegawa City
(Okegawa Station Nishi-guchi Park)

fig. 9
Work 98-N
1999年
アルミニウム、3M シート
440.0×300.0×420.0cm
HAT 神戸（灘の浜ファニチャーアート）

Work 98-N
1999
Aluminum, 3M sheet
440.0×300.0×420.0cm
HAT Kobe (Furniture Art of Nada Beach)

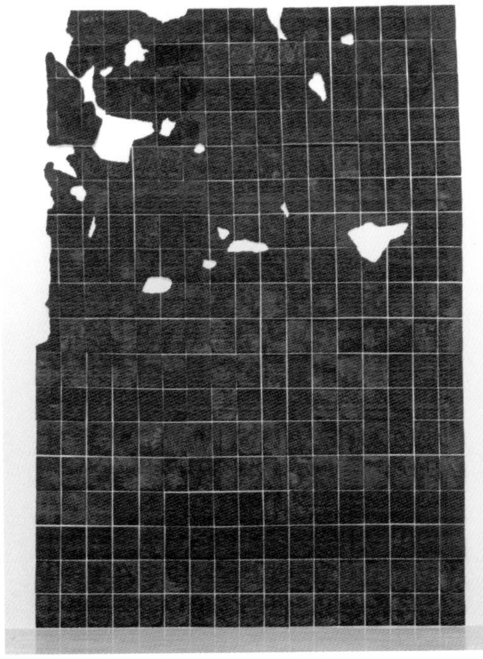

fig. 10
Newspaper 99-NG
1997年
アルミニウム合金、ステンレス鋼線材
755.0×520.0cm
個人蔵

Newspaper 99-NG
1997
Aluminum alloy, stainless steel
755.0×520.0cm
Private Collection

fig. 11
「三島喜美代—遊ぶ 見つめる 創りだす」展での
展示風景
(Copy '78-'80、Comic-07、バナナボックス、ニュースペーパー06、ニュースペーパー、リーフレット)
滋賀県立陶芸の森 陶芸館、岐阜県現代陶芸美術館

Exhibition view of "Mishima Kimiyo: Play Watch Create"
(*Copy '78-'80, Comic-07, Banana Box, Newspaper '06, Newspaper, Leaflet*)
The Shigaraki Ceramic Cultural Park, The Museum of Contemporary Ceramic Art, Museum of Modern Ceramic Art, Gifu

fig. 12
Newspaper (Work 2003)
2001-03年
溶融スラグ、陶
右：120.0×91.0×60.0cm
左：97.0×141.0×89.0cm
個人蔵

Newspaper (Work 2003)
2001-03
Melted slag, ceramic
Right: 120.0×91.0×60.0cm
Left: 97.0×141.0×89.0cm
Private Collection

fig. 13
Work 03
2002年
FRP、火山灰、彩色／陶、転写
インスタレーション（サイズ可変）
岐阜県現代陶芸美術館

Work 03
2002
FRP, volcanic ashes, hand-painted/silkscreen on ceramic
Installation (Dimension variable)
Museum of Modern Ceramic Art, Gifu

fig. 14
もうひとつの再生 2005-N
2005年
陶、転写、彩色
460.0×350.0×350.0cm
ベネッセアートサイト直島

Another Rebirth 2005-N
2005
Silkscreen and hand-painted on ceramic
460.0×350.0×350.0cm
Benesse Art Site Naoshima

fig. 15
Untitled
2006年
アルミニウム、転写
難波オリエンタルホテル

Untitled
2006
Silkscreen on aluminum
Namba Oriental Hotel

fig. 16
Work 2012
2012年
陶、転写、彩色
250.0×215.0×215.0cm
東横イン品川港南口天王洲アイル エントランス

Work 2012
2012
Silkscreen and hand-painted on ceramic
250.0×215.0×215.0cm
Toyoko Inn Tokyo Shinagawa konan-guchi
Tennozu Isle Entrance

fig. 17
Work 21-A
2021年
陶、転写、鉄
サイズ可変
森美術館

Work 21-A
2021
Silkscreen on ceramic, iron
Dimension variable
Mori Art Museum

fig. 18
Work 23-S
2023年
鉄、転写、彩色
青:220.0×260.0×250.0cm
赤:210.0×210.0×240.0cm
個人蔵

Work 23-S
2023
Silkscreen and hand-printed
on iron
Blue: 220.0×260.0×250.0cm
Red: 210.0×210.0×240.0cm
Private Collection

略年譜

【凡例】
・三島喜美代に関する事項は、『三島喜美代―遊ぶ 見つめる 創りだす』(岐阜県現代陶芸美術館、2023年)を主な参照源とし、作家親族のご助言による加筆のほか、追加調査を経て明らかとなったことを追補した。
・社会の出来事に関する事項は、東京美術倶楽部編『日本の20世紀芸術』(平凡社、2014年)から主要なものを抜粋し転載した。

西暦	年齢		社会の出来事
1932	0歳	12月10日、大阪府大阪市に志水喜代次、きぬ子の長女として生まれる。	1932年5月 五·一五事件 1936年2月 二·二六事件 1939年7月 国民徴用令が施行 1940年9月 日独伊三国同盟が成立 1941年 12月 日本軍が真珠湾を攻撃、太平洋戦争勃発 1945年8月 広島と長崎に原爆投下 日本、ポツダム宣言を受諾(敗戦)
1946	14歳	この頃から藤間流日本舞踊を習う	1946年 1月 昭和天皇による人間宣言 11月 独立美術協会展が再開 1950年6月 朝鮮戦争勃発

3歳頃の三島喜美代

まぁ、やんちゃだったもんですから。
まま事遊びなんかは、あんまりしたことがない。
お人形遊びもしたことない。
小さい時から虫を集めるのが好きで、
虫ばっかり飼っていました。

―「三島喜美代―人と作品―」岐阜県現代陶芸美術館、2005年(岐阜県現代陶芸美術館オリジナルビデオソフト)より―

藤間流日本舞踊を舞う三島喜美代

日本舞踊もやってたんですけど、人に教わってそのとおりやる、それが何か面白くなかったんですね。自分で振り付けして、とかそういうふうなことをやりたいな、と思ったんですけど、日本舞踊の場合、私だけでなしに三味線とか、いろいろな人に関わるので、それがちょっと煩わしいという感じだったんです。

―「三島喜美代は語る―ハンス・ウルリッヒ・オブリスト」『三島喜美代―Mishima Kimiyo』艸居、2021年より―

高等女学校時代の三島喜美代

小さいときは虫を飼って
顕微鏡で観察するのが好きだったので、
大きくなったら医者になりたいと思っていました。
でも母親に反対されたもんですから、
家で絵ばっかり描いていたんですね。

―「三島喜美代―人と作品―」岐阜県現代陶芸美術館、2005年(岐阜県現代陶芸美術館オリジナルビデオソフト)より―

西暦	年齢		社会の出来事

担任の先生、美術部の仲間と三島喜美代

受け持ちの絵の先生が「何を描いてもいいよ」って言われたんで。私が描いてもっていくと、「あ、このほうが面白いね」っていってくれるんで、ついつい、はまり込んでいってしまって。知らない間に美術の世界に入っていました。

―「三島喜美代インタビュー―2023年7月19日 大阪・十三のアトリエにて」『三島喜美代―遊ぶ 見つめる 創りだす』岐阜県現代陶芸美術館、2023年より―

西暦	年齢		社会の出来事
1951	19歳	大阪市立扇町高等女学校（現、大阪市立扇町高等学校）を卒業。	1951年 10月 サンフランシスコ講和条約・日米安全保障条約調印
1952	20歳	アトリエモンターニュ美術研究所に入所。同研究所主宰の三島茂司（1920-1985）に師事。	
1953	21歳	三島茂司と結婚。	

**毎日もう、朝から晩まで絵ばっかり
描いていました、2人で。
朝方の4時くらいまで描いてましたね。
いつも徹夜ですわ。**

―「三島喜美代―人と作品―」岐阜県現代陶芸美術館、2005年（岐阜県現代陶芸美術館オリジナルビデオソフト）より―

西暦	年齢		社会の出来事
1954	22歳	独立美術協会に所属する（以降1969年まで出展）。 「第22回独立展」に出品した《玉葱と壺》が関西独立展で独立奨励賞を受賞。	1954年 3月 第五福竜丸がビキニ環礁の水爆実験で被災

24歳頃の三島喜美代。三島茂司、長女の磨子と

西暦	年齢		社会の出来事
1958	26歳	独立美術協会の会友になる。	1959年 4月 皇太子明仁親王ご成婚
1961	29歳	「第29回独立展」で《執》と《跡》が大阪市賞を、関西独立展で関西独立同人賞を受賞。	1961年 4月 ソビエトのガガーリン、初の有人宇宙飛行に成功
1962	30歳	義兄が戦地から持ち帰った軍隊毛布や蚊帳、茂司が所有する外国の雑誌や新聞をコラージュした作品制作を開始。	1962年 10月 キューバ危機
1963	31歳	「第31回独立展」にコラージュ技法を取り入れた《天使・術》《天使・罪》《天使・詩》を出品し、独立賞・須田賞を受賞。 京都のギャラリー16で夫の茂司と初めての展覧会「三島茂司・三島喜美代二人展」を開催（1966年まで毎年開催）。	1963年 11月 ケネディ大統領暗殺

第31回独立展にて、独立賞・須田賞受賞作品の前で

西暦	年齢		社会の出来事
1964	32歳	国立近代美術館京都分館(現・京都国立近代美術館)で開催された「現代美術の動向 絵画と彫塑」に《Work-64-I》(no. 9)を出展。 「第32回独立展」に出品した《悪魔・呰》《悪魔・夢》が関西独立展で関西独立賞を受賞。 初めての個展を画廊あのにて開催。	1964年 10月 東京オリンピック開催
1965	33歳	印刷物をコラージュした《夜の詩 I》が「第9回シェル美術賞展」で佳作賞を受賞。	1965年 2月 アメリカ軍、北ベトナムへ爆撃開始
1966	35歳	「第1回毎日美術コンクール」で努力賞を受賞。 「第34回独立展」に《変貌 I》を出品。関西独立展で関西独立努力賞を受賞。	
1968	36歳	グタイピナコテカで開催された個展「アメリカ抽象画家サム・フランシス」のオープニングパーティーに出席。	1969年 7月 アポロ11号が月面着陸に成功
1970	38歳	この頃、シルクスクリーンで文字を陶に転写し焼成する作品制作に本格的に取り組む。 **新聞をコラージュした平面作品を制作していた時、床に転がっていたクチャクチャの新聞が凄く気になって。平面よりも立体の方が何かインパクトあるんじゃないかと。土はそれまで全然やったことがなかったんですけど、いっぺんやってみようと。** —「三島喜美代—人と作品—」岐阜県現代陶芸美術館、2005年(岐阜県現代陶芸美術館オリジナルビデオソフト)より—	1970年 光化学スモッグ発生
1971	39歳	「第1回日本陶芸展」の前衛部門で陶に新聞を転写した《包み》が入選。	
1972	40歳	イタリアの国際陶磁器博物館で開催された「第30回ファエンツア国際陶芸展」に参加(以降1980年まで出品)。	1972年 5月 沖縄、日本復帰
1973	41歳	「第2回日本陶芸展」前衛部門で《パッケージ—こわれもの注意》を出品。 **陶のパッケージは案外簡単にできて、それを発表したら意外に評判が良くて。それで2回目[第2回日本陶芸展]は段ボール箱に「われもの注意」のビラ貼ったり、そのままのを作ってみたんですね。すると搬入の時に「そこのゴミ早く捨てろ~」って声が聞こえてきて。あ、これは面白いと思ったんですよ。** —「三島喜美代—人と作品—」岐阜県現代陶芸美術館、2005年(岐阜県現代陶芸美術館オリジナルビデオソフト)より—	1973年 11月 第一次オイルショック
1974	42歳	「第32回ファエンツァ国際陶芸展」に出品した《Package》がゴールドメダルを受賞。 「第11回現代日本美術展」の公募部門で《Fragile》が佳作賞を受賞。	
1975	43歳	「第3回日本陶芸展」前衛部門で《包み》が入選。フランスから一時帰国していた菅井汲(1919-96)の助手として指導を受ける(1977年まで)。	1975年 4月 サイゴン陥落、ベトナム戦争終結 1976年 2月 ロッキード事件

西暦	年齢		社会の出来事

三島喜美代、十三のアトリエにて

小さいのばかり作っていると、なんか手仕事みたいで、思うようにポッと出来てしまうのが面白くなくなってきた。何か挑戦したくなって、拡大してガリバーみたいにすればどうなるかな、と思って。そのときフランスから菅井汲が帰ってきていて、相談したら「お〜やれやれ、絶対面白いよ!」と。それにふいっと乗ってしまったんですね。

—「三島喜美代—人と作品—」岐阜県現代陶芸美術館、2005年(岐阜県現代陶芸美術館オリジナルビデオソフト)より—

西暦	年齢		社会の出来事
1981	49歳	この頃、岐阜県土岐市で産業用窯を借りて制作を開始。	
1984	52歳	のちに《20世紀の記憶》(no. 82)となる作品制作に着手。耐火レンガの片面に、外国語の新聞記事を転写。	

1984年、土岐市のアトリエの庭にて

西暦	年齢		社会の出来事
1985	53歳	師であり、夫である三島茂司が逝去。享年65歳。	
1986	54歳	ロックフェラー財団(ACC)の奨学金でニューヨークに留学(1987年まで)。アンソニー・カロ(1924-2013)、ロイ・リキテンシュタイン(1923-97)、ルイーズ・ネヴェルソン(1899-1988)と交流。	1986年 4月 チェルノブイリ原子力発電所で爆発事故
1988	56歳	「第2回日本現代陶彫展」で《Package 88-T》(p. 167, fig. 3)が金賞を受賞。 この頃、岐阜県土岐市にアトリエを構える。	

土岐市のアトリエにて

西暦	年齢		社会の出来事
1989	57歳	「第2回国際陶磁器展美濃'89」で銅賞を受賞。	1989年 1月 昭和天皇が崩御、「平成」に改元 6月 天安門事件 11月 ベルリンの壁が取り壊される 12月 マルタ会談、アメリカ・ソビエトの冷戦終結 1990年 8月 東西ドイツが統一 1991年 1月 湾岸戦争が勃発 1993年 3月 皇太子徳仁親王ご成婚
1994	62歳	滋賀県立陶芸の森にある陶芸研修館(アート・イン・レジデンス)に招聘される。	1995年 1月 阪神淡路大震災 3月 地下鉄サリン事件
1996	64歳	「彩の国さいたま彫刻バラエティ'96」で《Newspaper97-A》(p. 170, fig. 8)が大賞を受賞。	
1998	66歳	阪神淡路大震災の復興事業で計画されたアートプロジェクト「HAT神戸 灘の浜ファニチャーアート」にて、排気筒を作品にした《Work 98-N》(p. 170, fig. 9)を発表。	
2000	68歳	この頃、産業廃棄物を1,400度で焼成したガラス状の粉末「溶融スラグ」を用いた作品を手がけはじめる。	
2001	69歳	「第19回現代日本彫刻展」で《Work-2001-U》が山口県立美術館賞と市民賞を受賞。 村松画廊の「三島喜美代展—情報の瓦礫展」に《20世紀の記憶》(no. 82)を出品。外国の新聞記事を転写した裏面に、1900年から2000年までの100年間のあいだに発刊された日本の新聞記事を転写(2013年完成)。	2001年 9月 アメリカ同時多発テロ
2002	70歳	「土岐市ユーモア彫刻展」で焼津市長賞を受賞。	

西暦	年齢		社会の出来事
2003	71歳	開いた漫画雑誌を伏せ置きにした溶融スラグによる作品(nos. 73-75)を制作。	
2005	73歳	瀬戸内海に浮かぶ直島に、ゴミ箱を巨大化した野外彫刻《もうひとつの再生 2005-N》(fig. 14)を設置。	
			2008年 9月 リーマン・ショック
			2011年 3月 東日本大震災
2015	83歳	三島喜美代のインスタレーション作品を常設展示する「ART FACTORY 城南島」が開設。 **複数の作品をまとめて見て頂く機会はなかなかありませんでした。広い空間の中で、これまでの作品を皆さんにお見せすることは私の長年の夢でした。** —ART FACTORY 城南島 プレスリリースより—	
2018	86歳	約50年振りとなる夫婦での展覧会「三島茂司 三島喜美代 二人展」が東京のMEMで開催。	
2019	87歳	世界文化遺産の清水寺 成就院で開催されたICOM京都大会記念展覧会「CONTACT つなぐ・むすぶ 日本と世界のアート展」で《Newspaper P-18A》と《Work 18-C13》を展示。	2019年 5月 皇太子徳仁親王が天皇に即位、「令和」に改元
		イタリアのアートフェア「アルティッシマ」でサルディーニャの芸術 バック・トゥ・ザ・フューチャーを受賞。 第5回安藤忠雄文化財団賞を受賞。 **今も変なものを作ろうと思ってわくわくしている。皆が「何やこれ」と言うのを聞きたい。** —「間奏曲 ゴミがモチーフ 消費文化問う」『読売新聞』、2019年6月13日夕刊より—	2020年 1月 新型コロナウィルスが世界的に拡大
2021	89歳	森美術館で開催された「アナザーエナジー展 挑戦しつづける力ー世界の女性アーティスト16人」に選出され出展。 令和3年度文化庁長官表彰を受賞。	2021年 8月 東京オリンピック・パラリンピック開催
2022	90歳	2021年度日本陶磁協会賞 金賞を受賞。 「第11回円空大賞展」にて円空賞を受賞。 第63回毎日芸術賞を受賞(美術I部門)。	2022年 2月 ロシアがウクライナに侵攻を開始
2023	91歳	岐阜県現代陶芸美術館で、過去から現在まで100点の作品を展示する大規模な個展「三島喜美代ー遊ぶ 見つめる 創りだす」が開催。	2023年 10月 パレスチナ・イスラエル戦争勃発
2024	92歳	練馬区立美術館で「三島喜美代ー未来への記憶」が開催。	

直島にて《もうひとつの再生 2005-N》除幕式

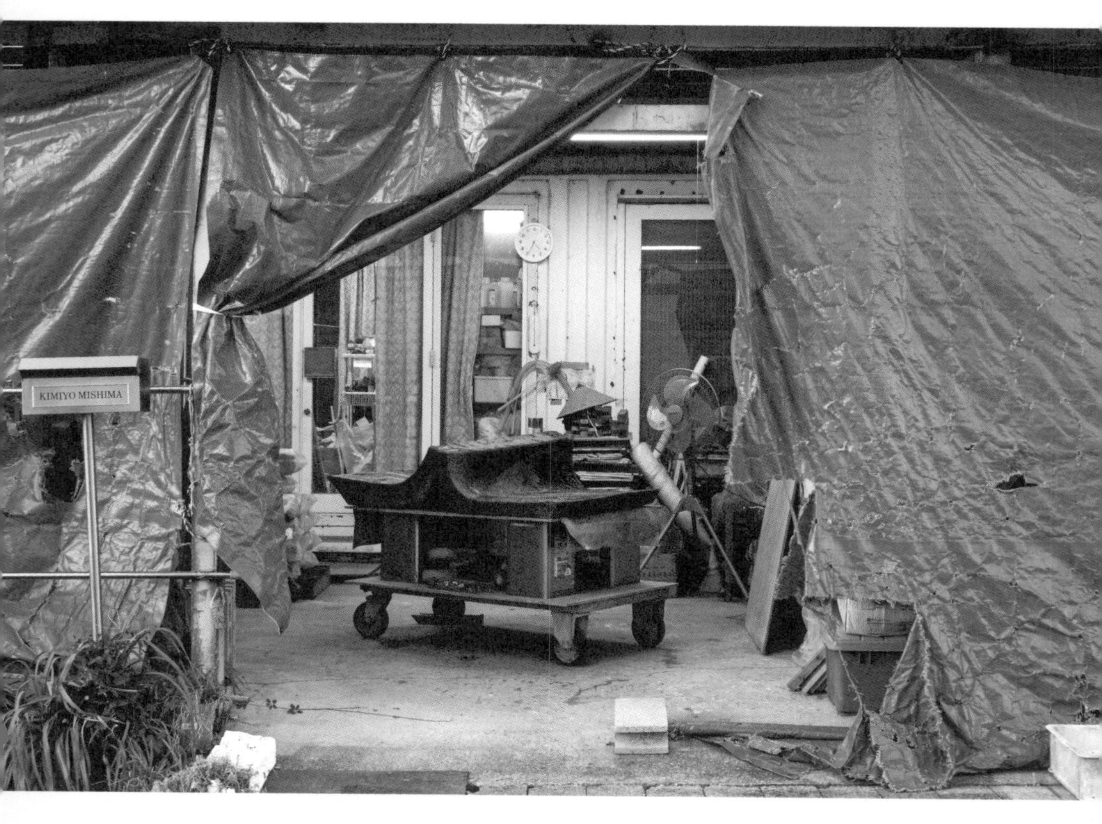
KIMIYO MISHIMA

Chronology

Notes

- Events related to the life and career of Mishima Kimiyo were mainly compiled based on the catalogue of the exhibition "Mishima Kimiyo: Play Watch Create" (Museum of Modern Ceramic Art, Gifu, 2023), and partly corrected/supplemented according to recommendations from the artist's family, or based on findings made through additional investigation.
- "General worldwide events" were selected from *The 20th Century Art in Japan* (Heibonsha, 2014) compiled by Tokyo Art Club.

Year	Age		General worldwide events
1932	0	Is born on December 10 in Osaka as the first daughter of Shimizu Kiyoji and Kinuko.	May 15 Incident / May 1932 February 26 Incident / February 1936 Enforcement of the National Requisition Ordinance / July 1939 Forming of an alliance between Japan, Germany and Italy / September 1940 Outbreak of the Pacific War after the Japanese military strikes Pearl Harbor / December 1941
1946	14	Begins to study Fujima School style Japanese dance.	Atomic bombings of Hiroshima and Nagasaki / August 1945 Acceptance by Japan of the Potsdam Declaration (of defeat) Humanity Declaration by Emperor Showa / January 1946 Resumption of the Dokuritsu Exhibition (Dokuritsu Art Association) / November 1946 Outbreak of the Korean War / June 1950

Photo: Mishima Kimiyo, age 3

I was a mischievous girl, and didn't do things like playing house much.
I also never played with dolls.
Since I was small, I liked to collect insects,
and I was always keeping some at home.

(from *Mishima Kimiyo: Person and Works,* original video of the Museum of Modern Ceramic Art, Gifu, 2005)

Photo: Mishima Kimiyo performs Fujima School style Japanese dance

I was also learning Nihonbuyo, which is a traditional Japanese dance. But the way that Japanese dance was taught was not very interesting to me because it's in a rigid form and style, and you have to follow and learn the certain forms, and you don't really have freedom for choreography. I think I would have had more fun in the Japanese traditional dancing if I had the free-dom to choreograph, but in order for those traditional dances to be on stage, you have to follow the rules. A lot of people are involved, not only the dancers but the musicians and a lot of other people working as a team and I'd have to follow certain rules, so I wasn't really a fan of that.

(from Hans Ulrich Obrist, "Mishima Kimiyo Speaks," *Mishima Kimiyo,* Sokyo, 2021)

Photo: Mishima Kimiyo as a high school student

As a little girl, I kept insects at home.
I liked to observe them under a microscope,
and I was dreaming of becoming a doctor.
But my mother objected, and I ended up
painting pictures at home all the time.

(from *Mishima Kimiyo: Person and Works,* original video of the Museum of Modern Ceramic Art, Gifu, 2005)

Photo: Mishima Kimiyo with her fellow art club students and teacher

My home room teacher told me that I was free to paint anything. When I showed him the paintings that I'd made at home, he said something like "These are rather interesting!" That encouraged me to paint more, and before I knew it, I was totally immersed in the world of art.

(from an interview with Mishima Kimiyo at Atelier Juso, Osaka, on July 19, 2023. Published in the catalog for "*Mishima Kimiyo: Play Watch Create,*" Museum of Modern Ceramic Art, Gifu, 2023)

Year	Age		General worldwide events
1951	19	Graduates from what is today Osaka Municipal Ogimachi General High School.	Signing of the San Francisco Peace Treaty and the US-Japan Security Treaty / October 1951
1952	20	Joins the art school Atelier Montagne, and studies under the school's teacher Mishima Shigeji (1920-1985).	
1953	21	Marries Mishima Shigeji. ***The two of us spent our days painting, from morning to night. We wouldn't stop until 4 in the morning. We always painted all night.*** (from *Mishima Kimiyo: Person and Works*, original video of the Museum of Modern Ceramic Art, Gifu, 2005)	
1954	22 Photo: Mishima Kimiyo at age 24, with Mishima Shigeji and their daughter Mako	Joins the Dokuritsu Bijutsu Kyokai [Dokuritsu Art Association] (and continues to participate in their exhibitions until 1969). *Onion and Pot*, shown at the 22nd Dokuritsu Exhibition, receives a Dokuritsu Encouragement Prize at the Kansai Dokuritsu Exhibition.	Nuclear test at the Bikini Atoll and exposure of the Daigo Fukuryu Maru to nuclear fallout / March 1954
1958	26	Becomes a fellow member of the Dokuritsu Bijutsu Kyokai.	Marriage of Crown Prince Naruhito / April 1959
1961	29	*Dedication* and *Trace* receive Osaka Citizen Prize at the 29th Dokuritsu Exhibition, and Kansai area Dokuritsu Prize at the Kansai Dokuritsu Exhibition.	First manned space flight accomplished by Soviet cosmonaut Yuri Gagarin / April 1961
1962	30	Starts making collages from army blankets and mosquito nets that her brother-in-law brought home from the battle front, as well as her husband Shigeji's foreign magazines and newspapers.	Cuban crisis / October 1962
1963	31 Photo: In front of her Dokuritsu Prize and Suda Prize winning works at the 31st Dokuritsu Exhibition	Presents *Angel-Technique*, *Angel-Guilt* and *Angel-Poem*, three works incpororating collage techniques, at the 31st Dokuritsu Exhibition, and receives a Dokuritsu Prize and Suda Prize. "Mishima Shigeji and Mishima Kimiyo Exhibition," her first exhibition together with her husband, is shown at gallery 16 in Kyoto (and is repeated annually until 1966).	Assassination of President Kennedy / November 1963
1964	32	Exhibits *Work-64-I* (no. 9) at the "Trends in Contemporary Japanese Painting and Sculpture" exhibition at Annex Museum of the National Museum of Modern Art, Tokyo (today The National Museum of Modern Art, Kyoto). *Devil-Fortress* and *Devil-Dream*, presented at the 32nd Dokuritsu Exhibition, receive Kansai area Dokuritsu Prize at the Kansai Dokuritsu Exhibition. Her first solo exhibition opens at Gallery Ano.	Opening of the Tokyo Olympics / 1964
1965	33	*Poem of Night I*, a collage of various printed matters, receives a honorable mention at the 9th Annual Shell Exhibition.	Start of the bombing of North Vietnam by the US Army / February 1965
1966	35	Receives a Effort Award at the 1st Mainichi Shimbun Art Conpetition. Shows *Transfiguration I* at the 34th Dokuritsu Exhibition, and receives a Kansai area Dokuritsu Effort Award at the Kansai Dokuritsu Exhibition.	
1968	36	Attends the opening party of an exhibition of works by the American abstract painter Sam Francis at Gutai Pinacotheca.	Landing of Apollo 11 on the Moon / July 1969

Year	Age		General worldwide events
1970	38	Begins to seriously employ the silkscreen technique to create works by transferring letters onto clay that she subsequently fires. ***When I was making two-dimensional newspapers collages, the crumpled newspapers scattered across the floor caught my attention. It appeared to me that three-dimensional works would make a stronger impact than two-dimensional ones. I had never worked with clay before, but I decided to give it a try.*** (from *Mishima Kimiyo: Person and Works*, original video of the Museum of Modern Ceramic Art, Gifu, 2005)	Occurrence of photochemical smog / 1970
1971	39	*Package*, a work for which she transferred a newspaper onto clay, is selected for the avant-garde section of the 1st Japan Ceramic Art Exhibition.	Return of Okinawa to Japan / May 1972
1972	40	Participates in the 30th International Ceramic Exhibition at the International Museum of Ceramics in Faenza, Italy (continuously until 1980).	Fist oil crisis / November 1973
1973	41	Shows *Package-Fragile* in the avant-garde section of the 2nd Japan Ceramic Art Exhibition. ***The clay work Package was easier to make than I had expected, and when I exhibited it, the response was surprisingly positive. So for the second Japan Ceramic Art Exhibition, I made another one for which I attached "Fragile" stickers to a cardboard box. While putting up the exhibits, someone asked me to "quickly dispose of that garbage," and I found that quite funny.*** (from *Mishima Kimiyo: Person and Works*, original video of the Museum of Modern Ceramic Art, Gifu, 2005)	
1974	42	Receives a Gold Medal for *Package* at the 32nd International Museum of Ceramics in Faenza. *Fragile* receives a honorable mention at the 11th Contemporary Art Exhibition of Japan.	Fall of Saigon and end of the Vietnam War / April 1975
1975	43 Photo: Mishima Kimiyo at Atelier Juso	*Package* is selected for the avant-garde section of the 3rd Japan Ceramic Art Exhibition. Studies under from Sugai Kumi (1919-1996) as his assistant during the artist's temporary return to Japan from France (until 1977). ***Getting bored with making small pieces that are easy to make like handiwork, I began to feel like doing something more challenging. Then I came up with the idea to try and blow things up to Gulliver kind of dimensions. Kumi Sugai had just returned from France at the time, and when talking to him, he found the idea exciting and encouraged me to go ahead with it. That's what I did.*** (from *Mishima Kimiyo: Person and Works*, original video of the Museum of Modern Ceramic Art, Gifu, 2005)	Lockheed bribery scandal / February 1976
1981	49	Starts making works using industrial kilns in Toki, Gifu.	

Year	Age		General worldwide events
1984	52	Commences work on what would eventually become *Memories of the 20th Century* (no. 82). For this work, she transfers foreign newspaper texts onto pieces of firebrick.	Opening of Tokyo Disneyland / April 1983
Photo: In the garden of her atelier in Toki, 1984			
1985	53	Her teacher and husband, Mishima Shigeji dies at the age of 65.	
1986	54	Studies in New York on a grant from the Rockefeller Foundation / ACC (until 1987), where she meets Anthony Caro (1924-2013), Roy Lichtenstein (1923-97) and Louise Nevelson (1899-1988).	Accident at the Chernobyl Nuclear Power Plant / April 1986
1988	56	*Package-88-T* (p. 167, fig. 3) receives a Golden Medal at the 2nd Contemporary Ceramics Art Exhibition.	
Photo: At her atelier in Toki		Sets up her atelier in Toki, Gifu, around this time.	
1989	57	Receives a Bronze Medal at the 2nd International Ceramics Festival Mino '89.	Passing of the Emperor Showa and beginning of the ""Heisei"" era / January 1989 Tiananmen Square protests / June 1989 Fall of the Berlin Wall / November 1989 Malta Summit and end of the Cold War / Decdember 1989
			Reunification of East and West Germany / August 1990
			Outbreak of the Gulf War / January 1991
			Marriage of the Imperial Prince Naruhito / March 1993
1994	62	Is invited to participate in the Shigaraki Ceramic Cultural Park's "Artist In Residence" program.	Great Hanshin-Awaji Earthquake / January 1995 Tokyo subway sarin attack / March 1995
1996	64	Receives a Grand Prize for *Newspaper 97-A* (p. 170, fig. 8) at "Sai no Kuni Chokoku Variety '96."	
1998	66	Unveils *Work 98-N* (p. 170, fig. 9), made from exhaust pipes, at "HAT Kobe Nada-no-hama Furniture Art," an art project that was part of the reconstruction activities after the Great Hanshin-Awaji Earthquake.	
2000	68	Starts creating works from vitrified melted slag by firing industrial waste at 1,400 degrees.	
2001	69	*Work-2001-U* wins the Yamaguchi Prefectural Art Museum Prize and a Citizen Award at the 19th Contemporary Ceramics Art Exhibition.	Synchronized terrorist attacks in New York / September 2001
		Shows *Memories of the 20th Century* (no. 82) at the exhibition "Mishima Kimiyo: The Debris of Information" at Muramatsu Gallery. On the reverse side of the work showing articles from foreign newspapers, she goes on to transfer articles from Japanese newspapers that were published between the years 1900 and 2000. (Work completed in 2013.)	
2002	70	Receives a Yaizu Mayer Prize at the 3rd Japan Humorous Pottery Sculpture Exhibition.	
2003	71	Makes works from melted slag (nos. 73-75) in the shapes of comic magazines opened and placed upside down.	

Year	Age		General worldwide events
2005	73	Installs *Another Rebirth 2005-N* (p. 173, fig. 14), a sculpture in the shape of a giant waste basket, on Naoshima, an island in the Seto Inland Sea.	Bankruptcy of Lehman Brothers / September 2008
Photo: Unveiling of *Another Rebirth 2005-N* at Naoshima			
2015	83	ART FACTORY Jonanjima opens as a facility with installations by Mishima Kimiyo on permanent display. ***As there had been few opportunities for people to see multiple works in one place, it was a longstanding dream of mine to show Mishima's previous works together in a spacious setting.*** (from ART FACTORY Jonanjima's press release)	Great East Japan Earthquake / March 2011
2018	86	"Mishima Shigeji + Mishima Kimiyo Exhibition," the first show of works by the pair in about 50 years, opens at MEM in Tokyo.	
2019	87	*Newspaper P-18A* and *Work 18-C13* are shown at "CONTACT," an exhibition commemorating ICOM Kyoto 2019, at the Jojuin Garden of the world heritage site Kiyomizu Temple. Receives a Sardi per l'Arte Back to the Future Prize at the "Artissima" art fair in italy. Receives the 5th Tadao Ando Cultural Foundation Award. ***I'm still eager and excited to make weird things. I want to hear people say, "What the heck is this?!"*** (from "Intermezzo: Garbage as a Motif – Questioning Consumer Culture" in *Yomiuri Shimbun*, evening edition, June 13, 2019)	Enthronement of the Imperial Prince Naruhito as Emperor, and beginning of the "Reiwa" era / May 2019 Outbreak and worldwide spread of COVID-19 / January 2020
2021	89	Is selected as an artist to exhibit works at "Another Energy: Power to Continue Challenging – 16 Women Artists from around the World" at Mori Art Museum. Receives a commendation from the Commissioner of the Agency for Cultural Affairs for the year 2021.	Tokyo Olympics and Paralympics / August 2021
2022	90	Receives the Japan Ceramic Society Award, Gold Medal, for the year 2021. Receives an Enku Award at the 11th Enku Grand Award Exhibition. Receives the 63rd Mainichi Art Award (Art Category I).	Invasion of Ukraine by Russia / February 2022
2023	91	"Mishima Kimiyo: Play Watch Create," a large-scale solo exhibition of 100 works from the past up to the present, is shown at the Museum of Modern Ceramic Art, Gifu.	Outbreak of the war between Palestine and Israel / October 2023
2024	92	The exhibition "Mishima Kimiyo: Memories for the Future" is shown at Nerima Art Museum.	

展覧会歴

町野陽輝・新井晃編

【凡例】
・本展覧会歴は三島喜美代の展覧会歴を、「個展」「グループ展」に分けて一覧表にしたものである。
・『三島喜美代―遊ぶ 見つめる 創りだす』(岐阜県現代陶芸美術館、2023年)を主に参照し、親族による加筆と追加調査により明らかとなった事項を追補した。
・翌年以降に同じタイトルの展覧会に出品がある場合は、展覧会名の後に( )で開催年を記した。
・会期、展覧会名、会場が不明なものは空欄とし、会場が特定できないものについては開催地のうしろに「*」をつけた。
・複数会場を巡回する展覧会については第1会場の会期のみを記した。
・アートフェアについては三島喜美代の単独展示に限って記載した。

個展

開催年	会期	展覧会名	会場
1964年		三島喜美代展(1965－68年、1970年)	画廊あの／大阪
1967年	10月23日－10月29日	三島喜美代作品展	ギャラリー16／京都
1968年	5月27日－6月2日	三島喜美代展	ギャラリー16／京都
1969年	7月14日－7月19日	三島喜美代 小品展	今橋画廊／大阪
1970年	6月9日－6月14日	三島喜美代展	ギャラリー16／京都
1971年			藤美画廊／大阪
1972年			今井画廊／大阪
	7月17日－7月23日	三島喜美代展	村松画廊(第二会場)／東京
1974年	2月18日－2月28日	三島喜美代展	南画廊／東京
1980年	1月15日－2月2日	三島喜美代作品展	ギャラリー16／京都
	4月7日－4月19日	三島喜美代展	桜画廊／愛知
1985年	3月1日－3月24日	三島喜美代展	ギャラリー上田・ウェアハウス／東京
1988年	9月27日－10月9日	三島喜美代展	ギャラリー16／京都
1989年	7月24日－8月5日	三島喜美代展―化石になった情報	村松画廊／東京
1990年	11月5日－11月7日	三島喜美代展―小品	ギャルリ・プス／東京
	9月3日－9月28日	三島喜美代展―クレイ・クレイジー	INAXギャラリー2／東京 INAXギャラリー／大阪
1992年	11月2日－11月21日	三島喜美代展	カサハラ画廊／大阪
1994年	3月14日－3月24日	コレクションによる三島喜美代展	ギャルリ・プス／東京
1998年	4月7日－4月19日	三島喜美代展	アートフロントギャラリー／東京 ヒルサイド・ギャラリー／東京
1999年	9月1日－9月28日	三島喜美代展―クレイジー・ペーパー	INAXギャラリー2／東京
2001年			株式会社ミキモト／東京
	9月25日－10月19日	三島喜美代展―情報の瓦礫(20世紀の記録)	村松画廊／東京
2004年	9月16日－10月12日	三島喜美代展―1960年代の平面	伊勢現代美術館
	7月1日－7月16日	三島喜美代展―1960年代の平面	ギャラリー新居／大阪、東京
2011年	5月26日－5月29日	三島喜美代	ART HK 11:MEMブース／香港
2013年	11月9日－12月14日	三島喜美代 Painting Period―1954-1970	ギャラリーヤマキファインアート／兵庫
2014年	11月29日	三島喜美代展プレオープン	ART FACTORY 城南島
2015年	12月5日－2016年2月28日	三島喜美代展[以降常設展示]	ART FACTORY 城南島

2016年	3月11日－4月9日	Mishima Kimiyo	タカ・イシイギャラリー／ニューヨーク
	3月24日－3月26日	Mishima Kimiyo	アート・バーゼル香港2016 （MEMブース）／香港
2017年	2月22日－2月26日	三島喜美代展	CoSTUME NATIONAL-LAB： ミツイ・ファイン・アーツ／東京
	5月2日－5月28日	Mishima Kimiyo	艸居／京都
	5月5日－5月7日	MISHIMA Kimiyo	フリーズ・ニューヨーク （ギャラリーヤマキファインアートブース） ／ニューヨーク
	9月2日－9月30日	三島喜美代	ギャラリーヤマキファインアート／兵庫
	10月7日－11月5日	三島喜美代展—Early Works	MEM／東京
	11月9日－11月12日	三島喜美代	ART021（艸居ブース）／上海
2018年	5月18日－6月14日	Mishima Kimiyo—Paintings	ノナカ・ヒル／ロサンゼルス
	6月8日－7月13日	MISHIMA KIMIYO—Paintings and Sculptures	アンヌ・モッセリ＝マルリギャラリー／ バーゼル
	9月1日－9月28日	MISHIMA KIMIYO Works since the Painting Period— 1970-	ギャラリーヤマキファインアート／兵庫
2019年	11月1日－11月3日	三島喜美代	アルティッシマ 2019（艸居ブース）／トリノ
2020年	1月16日－1月19日	三島喜美代	タイペイ ダンダイ（艸居ブース）／台北
	3月14日－7月5日	三島喜美代展	MEM／東京
	10月3日－10月31日	三島喜美代展	ギャラリーヤマキファインアート／兵庫
	10月24日－12月12日	Mishima Kimiyo	SOKYO Lisbon／リスボン
	12月24日－2021年3月7日	2020年度第4回コレクション展 —特集 三島喜美代	京都国立近代美術館
2021年	1月27日－2月27日	三島喜美代	艸居アネックス／京都
	2月9日－3月21日	Mishima Kimiyo	SHOP タカ・イシイギャラリー／香港
	7月15日－9月4日	三島喜美代—1950年代から2021年まで	SOKYO ATSUMI／東京
	9月21日－10月6日	三島喜美代展—パピエ・コレ	MEM／東京
2022年	1月29日－2月8日	三島喜美代展	銀座蔦屋書店
2023年	2月2日－4月26日	三島喜美代	艸居／京都
	9月16日－11月26日	三島喜美代—遊ぶ 見つめる 創りだす	岐阜県現代陶芸美術館
2024年	2月15日－4月17日	三島喜美代	艸居、艸居アネックス／京都
	5月19日－7月7日	三島喜美代展—未来への記憶	練馬区立美術館

グループ展

開催年	会期	展覧会名	会場
1954年		第22回独立展（第23－37回：1955－69年）	東京都美術館
		関西独立展（1955－69年）	大阪市立美術館
1961年		独立新人選抜展（1962－70年）	東京都美術館
1962年		朝日新人展	大阪高島屋百貨店、京都高島屋百貨店

		第1回モンターニュ展 (第2−5回:1963−66年)	モール・ギャラリー/京都 大阪画廊
1963年	10月	三島茂司・三島喜美代二人展(1964−66年)	ギャラリー16/京都
1964年	3月4日−3月15日	ギャラリー16新人展	都ホテル/京都
	4月4日−5月10日	現代美術の動向—絵画と彫塑展	国立近代美術館京都分館
	11月20日−11月27日	第3回国際青年美術家展—ヨーロッパ・日本展	池袋西武百貨店SSSホール
1965年	9月10日−9月25日	第9回シェル美術賞展	白木屋/東京
1966年		第1回毎日美術コンクール展	京都市美術館
1967年	3月4日−3月14日	第4回国際青年美術家展—アメリカ・日本展	池袋西武百貨店SSSホール
1968年		茨木現代美術展	茨木市民会館
1971年		第1回日本陶芸展(前衛部門)[北米に巡回] (第2−5回:1973年[中南米に巡回]、 1975、1977、1979年)	大丸百貨店/東京 岡山総合文化センター 愛知県美術館ほか巡回
1972年		第30回ファエンツァ国際陶芸展 (第31−38回:1973−80年)	ファエンツァ国際陶芸博物館
	6月6日−6月11日	10年目のギャラリー16展	ギャラリー16/京都
	10月19日−10月21日	第1回芦屋川国際ビエンナーレ展	ルナホール/兵庫
1973年		カルガリー国際陶芸展	カルガリー*
		第1回中日国際陶芸展	名古屋三越百貨店
	8月18日−10月14日	国際カップ展	日本海博アート・ミュージアム/石川
1974年		第2回芦屋川国際ビエンナーレ展	滴翠美術館/兵庫
	5月10日−5月30日	第11回日本国際美術展	東京都美術館、京都市美術館
1975年		現代日本版画展	フェラーラ近代美術館
	1月5日−1月19日	アート・ナウ'75	兵庫県立近代美術館
	1月18日−2月2日	現代美術四半世紀展 1950-1975	東京セントラル美術館
	5月10日−5月30日	第11回現代日本美術展(公募部門)	東京都美術館、京都市美術館
	9月24日−9月30日	第8回現代の造形 喜怒哀楽 現代美術50人展	大丸百貨店/京都
1976年		第11回ジャパン・アート・フェスティバル	上野の森美術館/東京 ワシントン州立大学附属美術館
		第6回クラクフ国際版画ビエンナーレ	クラクフ国立美術館
		現代日本陶芸展—白熱の中の創造	オーストラリア*、ニュージーランド*
		第12回現代日本美術展	東京都美術館
	6月13日−9月12日	第5回イギリス国際版画ビエンナーレ (第6回:1979年)	カートライトホール/ブラッドフォード
	9月1日−10月31日	日本陶磁名品展(1977年)	ロストック市立美術館 ドレスデン国立美術館
1977年	4月22日−4月27日	第1回日本現代版画大賞展	銀座松屋百貨店
1978年		大阪を中心にみる陶芸新地図	大阪府民ギャラリー
	6月3日−6月28日	女性作家招待展・日本	A.I.R ギャラリー/ニューヨーク
	8月24日−9月17日	現代日本の工芸展	京都国立近代美術館
	9月12日−9月17日	現代の工芸作家展	京都市美術館

1979年	4月14日－5月20日	現代工芸展—京都国立近代美術館蔵	群馬県立近代美術館
	4月21日－6月10日	日本陶芸の現在—京都国立近代美術館より	デンバー美術館
	8月8日－8月20日	志水楠男と作家たち展	南画廊／東京
1980年	5月24日－7月13日	カップで考える—あそびのやきもの国際展	北海道立近代美術館
	7月－9月	第7回ヴァロリス国際陶芸展	マニエリ美術館・陶器館／ヴァロリス
	7月25日－9月23日	まがいものの光景—現代美術とユーモア展	国立国際美術館／大阪
	10月25日－11月10日	クレイワーク—焼き物から造形へ（1981年）	大津西武百貨店 西武ホール 池袋西武百貨店
	10月26日－11月23日	1980 日本の版画	栃木県立美術館
1981年		日華現代陶芸展	国立台湾歴史博物館
		遊びの世界—もう一つのデザイン	大阪デザインセンター
	3月7日－3月29日	アート・ナウ 1970-1980	兵庫県立近代美術館
	11月1日－11月7日	諷刺とユーモア 今日の絵馬展	駅ビルかわさき
1982年		現代の日本の陶芸	ファエンツァ＊、ローマ＊、 ケベック国立美術館、香港芸術館
	2月11日－2月23日	くらしのなかのアート展	東急百貨店コミュニケーションスペース
	4月17日－5月9日	現代の陶芸 I—いま、土と火でなにが可能か	山口県立美術館
	4月27日－5月5日	視覚のサーカス—イリュージョン展 （－1983年）	銀座松屋百貨店 静岡伊勢丹百貨店 横浜高島屋百貨店ほか巡回
	9月7日－9月12日	第3回国際インパクトアート・フェスティバル （第4回：1983年［ソウルに巡回］）	京都市美術館
1983年		机上のニューヨーク展	西武エンジンルーム／東京
		標本箱展—時代を標本する	ソニービル／東京
		アーティスト国際ブック展1983	みやざき画廊／大阪
		ミニアチュール展	アークビル／京都 サンフランシスコ近代美術館
	6月29日－9月25日	日本美術の現在	ジュネーヴ美術・歴史博物館
	10月4日－12月4日	現代のリアリズム展	埼玉県立近代美術館
1984年		セラミックス×27展	ギャラリー・キアリトハザ／ブダペスト
		あそびのコレクション	ギャラリー上田／東京
		日本・現代陶芸展	マヤ・ベン画廊／チューリッヒ
		セラミック・トゥデイ（1985年）	池袋西武百貨店ガレリア 粋工芸画廊
1985年		Kitsch展	番画廊／大阪
		現代陶芸作家120人展	椿山荘／東京ほか開催
		ブック・セルフ・スカルプチャー	ギャラリー16／京都
		アーティスト・ブック展	フランクリン・ファーネスギャラリー／ ニューヨーク フジテレビギャラリー／東京
		KIS' 85 郡山国際美術展	郡山国立大学附設現代美術館
	4月20日	山村コレクション展	国立国際美術館／大阪

	5月13日－5月25日	作家による創作本展	みやざき画廊／大阪
	7月13日－8月4日	第10回シュピーツ陶芸展	シュピーツ＊
	8月16日－8月28日	世界ユーモア・カップ展 遊びのやきもの	小田急百貨店／東京
	9月2日－9月14日	第3回大阪現代アートフェア'85	大阪府立現代美術センター
	9月7日－9月21日	現代陶芸への招待展 Part I	ギャラリーいそがや／東京
	10月5日－11月4日	環境としてのイメージ— 開館15周年記念明日の美術館を求めて（II）	兵庫県立近代美術館
	10月21日－11月12日	ひとひらの、大地に寄す —アフリカ救済チャリティ展	ギャラリーいそがや／東京
	12月7日－1986年1月26日	1985 日本の版画展	栃木県立美術館
1986年		セラミック・ナウ	西武画廊／東京
		クレイワーク'86—イメージを注ぐ	ギャラリーマロニエ／京都
		読む物質・文字と物質	ギャラリー射手座／京都
		現代陶芸展	ブダペスト＊
	1月2日－1月26日	土・イメージと形体 1981-85	大津西武ホール 有楽町アート・フォーラム
	5月9日－7月4日	日本現代陶芸展	エヴァーソン美術館／シラキュース
	6月23日－6月29日	ESTIU Japó '86	ガローチャ博物館／オロット
	7月29日－9月21日	収蔵作品展・中期　日本の版画	東京都美術館
1987年	1月6日－2月11日	土と炎展—今日の造形 新たな展開と可能性	岐阜県美術館
	3月6日－3月27日	版画の世界2—シルクスクリーン	北海道立近代美術館
	5月9日－5月27日	オブジェ—逸脱する物質	つかしんホール／兵庫
1988年		ヨーロッパのコーヒーカップ展	ブリュッセル＊
		国島征二と2人展	インファッション阪急／ロサンゼルス
		ドローイング展	ギャラリークオーレ／大阪
	7月－8月	第9回国際ビエンナーレ	リモージュ＊
	9月2日－9月13日	手で見る美術展	有楽町アートフォーラム つかしんホール／兵庫、大分県立芸術館
	9月10日－10月9日	東西現代陶芸展 オリンピック・アート・ フェスティバル	韓国文化芸術振興院美術会館／ソウル
	9月15日－9月30日	第2回日本現代陶彫展'88	土岐市文化プラザ／岐阜
1989年		新規収蔵品展	栃木県立美術館
	2月2日－3月25日	現代美術の展開—収蔵作品による	東京都美術館
	2月20日－2月25日	主張するオブジェ展'89	信濃橋画廊／大阪
	3月4日－3月23日	幻の山村コレクション	兵庫県立近代美術館
	6月17日－7月23日	アート・エキサイティング'89—現在を超えて	埼玉県立近代美術館 クイーンズランド・アートギャラリー
	7月11日－7月23日	Back and Forth—高橋元尚・野村耕・ 三島喜美代 1960年代のコラージュ	ギャラリー16／京都
	10月1日－10月29日	京都の美術 昨日・きょう・明日 III —野村耕・三島喜美代と所蔵品	京都市美術館
	10月22日－11月5日	第2回国際陶磁器展美濃'89	多治見市総合体育館

1990年	5月11日－5月16日	朝日現代クラフト展（1992、1997年）	梅田阪急百貨店 有楽町阪急百貨店
	7月29日－9月16日	土の造形	栃木県立美術館
	10月5日－12月1日	現代の土展	東京都美術館
	10月6日－10月28日	現代の陶芸1980-1990 —関西の作家を中心として	和歌山県立近代美術館
1991年	4月20日－5月26日	変貌する陶芸—国際現代陶芸展	滋賀県立陶芸の森 陶芸館
	8月10日－10月6日	現代の美術'91—素材はいろいろ	徳島県立近代美術館
1992年		現代日本陶芸展	エヴァーソン美術館／シラキュース
		1992 現代陶芸国際招待展	国立台湾歴史博物館／台北
	6月2日－6月7日	美術選抜展	京都市美術館
	8月5日－8月30日	子供と造形—こどもの見た現代美術展	芦屋市立美術博物館
	9月16日－9月30日	カサハラ画廊20周年記念展	カサハラ画廊／大阪
1993年		リアルな美術・幻想の美術	東京都美術館
	3月2日－4月18日	京都国立近代美術館創立30周年記念 —世界の工芸展	京都国立近代美術館
	7月16日－8月22日	現代の陶芸 1950-1990	愛知県美術館
	8月27日－9月23日	珠玉のコレクション—開館60周年記念特別展	京都市美術館
	10月2日－12月5日	現代陶芸うつわ考 —視線はいつも暮らしの角度で	埼玉県立近代美術館
	12月12日－1994年3月21日	反復と増殖—現代美術のかたち	東京都美術館
1994年	2月8日－3月27日	現代美術の軌跡—1960-70年代の美術	東京都美術館
1995年		国際現代陶芸展	滋賀県立陶芸の森 陶芸館
		ファエンツアの風景・日本人受賞者展	土岐市セラトピア
		マジカルな視点	枚方市御殿山生涯学習美術センター
	4月19日－6月4日	戦後文化の軌跡 1945-1995展	目黒区美術館、広島市現代美術館 兵庫県立近代美術館ほか巡回
1996年		彩の国さいたま彫刻バラエティ'96（1998）	桶川駅西口公園／埼玉
	4月20日－7月7日	現代日本の陶彫作家展	彫刻の森美術館／神奈川
	11月23日－12月27日	戦後美術の断面—兵庫県立近代美術館所蔵 山村コレクションから	千葉市美術館
1997年	2月1日－3月24日	あるコレクターが見た現代美術 —山村コレクション展	兵庫県立近代美術館
	3月－1998年3月	日本の美術・世界の美術—この50年の歩み	東京都現代美術館
1998年		The Hope II	safaギャラリー／ブダペスト、ハンガリアン 写真美術館／ケチケメイト
	9月24日－11月15日	日本・ブラジル国際巡回現代美術展98-99	サンパウロ美術館 リオデジャネイロ近代美術館
1999年		プレート展	ストラスクラウド大学附属 コリンズ・ギャラリー／ロンドン
	2月16日－3月28日	関西の戦後美術 1950's-1990's	和歌山県立近代美術館
	10月8日－12月12日	イメージのむこうがわ展	東京都現代美術館

2000年		国際陶芸展	ケラミオン現代陶芸美術館／フレッヒェン
2001年	7月12日－11月11日	第19回現代日本彫刻展	宇部市野外彫刻美術館
2002年		イメージング・ザ・ブック現代美術館	アレキサンドリア図書館
	7月20日－9月1日	こどもとおとなの美術入門 変身アート展	群馬県立近代美術館
	10月12日－2003年1月19日	開館記念展Ⅰ現代陶芸の100年展 —第1部 日本陶芸の展開	岐阜県現代陶芸美術館
	10月20日－11月04日	第3回土岐市ユーモア陶彫展'02	セラトピア土岐 美術ギャラリー
2003年	7月11日－9月21日	あるサラリーマン・コレクションの軌跡 —戦後日本美術の場所（－2004年）	周南市美術博物館、三鷹市美術ギャラリー、福井県立美術館
	10月9日－11月25日	大地の芸術 クレイワーク新世紀展	国立国際美術館／大阪
2004年	5月24日－6月29日	現代のコデックス—陶磁器と本	セントラル・ミシガン大学マウントプレザントほかアメリカ巡回
2005年		日本の美術・世界の美術—この50年の歩み	東京都現代美術館
	1月13日－4月10日	私の風景	池田20世紀美術館／静岡
	4月16日－6月19日	謎なぞ美術展	浜田市世界こども美術館
	6月19日－9月25日	日本の現代陶芸・海外の現代陶芸 —迫力の時代	滋賀県立陶芸の森 陶芸館
	7月24日－9月11日	前衛の女性 1950-1975	栃木県立美術館
	10月7日－2006年7月9日	日本現代陶芸展	ボストン美術館、ジャパン・ソサエティ／ニューヨーク
2006年	1月21日－3月21日	日本の陶芸100年の精華	茨城県陶芸美術館
	4月25日－8月13日	リアル—陶芸に見るそれぞれの現実	岐阜県現代陶芸美術館
	11月17日－2007年2月26日	日本陶芸の伝統と前衛	セーヴル国立陶磁器美術館
2007年		メキシコー日本 彫刻の友愛展	モンテホ通り／メリダ
	5月25日－7月1日	描かれたことば	京都市美術館
	6月10日－9月24日	魅せられる…今、注目される日本の陶芸展 （－2012年）	滋賀県立陶芸の森 陶芸館 ニューオータニ美術館 静岡アートギャラリーほかアメリカ巡回
	11月8日－12月15日	型を破る	ジョアン・マービス画廊／ニューヨーク
	12月23日－2008年3月28日	前衛芸術の諸相	岐阜県現代陶芸美術館
2008年	3月1日－3月20日	大阪アート・カレイドスコープ展2008 —大阪時間	大阪府立現代美術センター
2009年	8月22日－9月23日	トリックアートの世界（－2011年）	豊橋市美術館、北海道釧路芸術館、三重県立美術館ほか巡回
2010年	4月－12月	OAP彫刻の小径2010—Un-Syntax	アートコートギャラリー／大阪
	11月2日－12月5日	ザ・ニュースペーパーズ	神田日勝記念美術館／北海道
	11月20日－2011年1月23日	これは本ではない—ブックアートの広がり	うらわ美術館、福井市美術館
2011年	9月2日－9月23日	日本×ファエンツァ—やきものの現在	イタリア文化会館／東京、多治見市文化工房ギャラリーヴォイス
2012年	3月3日－7月6日	陶芸の魅力×アートのドキドキ（－2013年）	滋賀県立陶芸の森 陶芸館、岐阜県現代陶芸美術館、兵庫陶芸美術館
	4月21日－6月27日	国際交流基金コレクション —日本陶芸、世界を巡る	茨城県陶芸美術館

	4月21日−8月19日	2012年春展—ポップ・命を抱いて	岐阜県現代陶芸美術館
	8月22日−9月22日	言葉と美術が繋ぐもの —中原佑介へのオマージュ	ギャラリーヤマキファインアート／兵庫
2013年	12月21日−2014年2月11日	物質(モノ)と美術	和歌山県立近代美術館
2014年	5月9日−5月28日	潮流—日本の現代美術	クリスティーズ／香港
	7月5日−8月24日	アイデンティティとオリジナリティ —現代陶芸新収蔵品展	兵庫陶芸美術館
	8月1日−9月15日	美術館でわぁお‼わくわくアート×クラフト	浦添市美術館
2015年	1月17日−4月4日	古代から現代—日本現代陶芸とその起源	サン・アントニオ美術館／オースティン
	6月13日−8月30日	きになるかたち展	岐阜県現代陶芸美術館
2016年	1月25日−2月21日	クロニクル、クロニクル!(2018年)	クリエイティブセンター大阪
2017年	2月4日−3月26日	開館30周年記念 ハコビ・グランド・コレクション —文字と記号セレクション	北海道立函館美術館
	3月21日−2018年11月25日	Show Me the Mini	フロリダ大学サミュエル・P・ハーン美術館
	4月18日−6月18日	コレクション×クロニクル—制作年からみる 岐阜県現代陶芸美術館コレクション	岐阜県現代陶芸美術館
	4月24日−5月31日	京畿世界陶磁ビエンナーレ —叙事・暮らしを歌う	利川世界陶磁センター
	6月9日−7月29日	激しい絵画—歴史的調査	ステファン・フリードマン・ギャラリー／ ロンドン
	7月15日−9月18日	2D プリンターズ展—芸術 —世界の承認をめぐる闘争について	栃木県立美術館
2018年	1月13日−3月10日	超絶技巧の日本	ケルン日本文化会館ほか巡回
	3月24日−4月15日	三島茂司 三島喜美代 二人展	MEM／東京
	11月3日−2019年1月20日	コレクション2—80年代の時代精神 (ツァイトガイスト)から	国立国際美術館／大阪
2019年	3月29日−6月16日	リニューアルオープン記念展 百年の編み手 たち—流動する日本の近現代美術	東京都現代美術館
	8月3日−9月29日	集めた!日本の前衛 —山村徳太郎の眼 山村コレクション展	兵庫県立美術館
	9月1日−9月8日	CONTACT つなぐ・むすぶ —日本と世界のアート展	清水寺 成就院／京都
2020年	2月6日−11月20日	心の傷—芸術とトラウマについて	ザ・ウェアハウス／ダラス
	9月5日−10月4日	モノとコトとカラダをめぐって—6つの視点	MEM／東京
	9月19日−11月8日	芦屋の時間 大コレクション展	芦屋市立美術博物館
2021年	4月22日−2022年1月16日	アナザーエナジー展 —挑戦しつづける力 世界の女性アーティスト 16人	森美術館／東京
	5月9日−7月4日	浮桟橋—ポストモダンと現代日本の陶芸	エヴァーソン美術館／シラキュース
	6月15日−7月4日	SPUR by MEM	MEM／東京
	10月15日−2022年2月6日	炎—陶磁器の時代	パリ市立近代美術館
	11月13日−2022年2月23日	MOTコレクション Journals 日々、記す vol.2	東京都現代美術館
	12月4日−2022年4月25日	第10回アジア・パシフィック・トリエンナーレ	クイーンズランド・アートギャラリー
2022年	2月5日−3月27日	20世紀からおみやげ。近代美術のたのしみ	和歌山県立近代美術館

	4月9日ー9月6日	ポーラ美術館開館20周年記念展 モネからリヒターへ—新規収蔵作品を中心に	ポーラ美術館／神奈川
	4月16日ー5月14日	GYFA ショー PART II —戦後の女性アーティスト 1970-2017展	ギャラリーヤマキファインアート／兵庫
	4月20日ー8月28日	身体と文体—今日の芸術 パリ市立近代美術館による近年の新規収蔵 作品から	パリ市立近代美術館
	8月15日ー9月25日	ヴォイド オブ ニッポン77 —戦後美術史のある風景と反復進行	GYLE／東京
	11月14日ー11月19日	2021年度 日本陶磁協会賞・金賞受賞記念 —桑田卓郎・三島喜美代展	壺中居／東京
	11月23日ー2023年1月29日	コレクション展	伊勢現代美術館
2023年	1月20日ー3月5日	第11回円空大賞展 共鳴—継承と創造	岐阜県美術館
	4月28日ー7月2日	Re: スタートライン—1963-1970/2023 現代美術の動向展シリーズにみる 美術館とアーティストの共感関係	京都国立近代美術館
	5月23日ー9月10日	MOMATコレクション	東京国立近代美術館
	6月13日ー7月2日	The Great Wall 1963-1970 開廊時の作家の表現	ギャラリー16／京都
	9月30日ー2024年2月25日	TAKEUCHI COLLECTION—心のレンズ展	WHAT MUSEUM／東京
	12月16日ー2024年1月3日	ラディカル・クレイ—日本の現代女性 アーティスト	シカゴ美術館

Selected Exhibitions

Compiled by Machino Haruki and Arai Hikaru

Notes

- The list of past exhibitions of works by Mishima Kimiyo is divided into "Solo Exhibitions" and "Group Exhibitions."
- While basically referencing the catalogue for "*Mishima Kimiyo: Play Watch Create*" (Museum of Modern Ceramic Art, Gifu, 2023), the list has been updated according to notes from the artist's family, or based on the results of additional investigation.
- For repeated displays of works at the same serial exhibition in the year(s) following the initial exhibition, the respective year(s) is/are indicated in parentheses after the exhibition title.
- Dates, titles and/or venues of exhibitions are not indicated where the respective data are unknown. Exhibitions at locations that are not clearly identifiable, are marked with an asterisk (*).
- For traveling exhibitions (at multiple locations), dates are indicated for the initial exhibition only. Information on all subsequent exhibitions is abbreviated
- For Art Fair, only the respective of Mishima Kimiyo's exhibitions are listed.

Solo Exhibitions

Year	Dates	Title	Venue
1964		Mishima Kimiyo (1965-68, 1970)	Gallery Ano / Osaka
1967	Oct. 23—Oct. 29	Mishima Kimiyo's Works Exhibition	galerie 16 / Kyoto
1968	May 27—Jun. 2	Mishima Kimiyo Exhibition	galerie 16 / Kyoto
1969	Jul. 14— Jul. 19	Mishima Kimiyo Small Works Exhibition	Imabashi Gallery / Osaka
1970	Jun. 9—Jun. 14	Mishima Kimiyo Exhibition	galerie 16 / Kyoto
1971			Fujimi Gallery / Osaka
1972		Mishima Kimiyo	Imai Gallery / Osaka
	Jul. 17—Jul. 23	Mishima Kimiyo	Muramatsu Gallery (2nd Venue) / Tokyo
1974	Feb. 18—Feb. 28	MISHIMA KIMIYO	Minami Gallery / Tokyo
1980	Jan. 15—Feb. 2	Mishima Kimiyo's Works Exhibition	galerie 16 / Kyoto
	Apr. 7—Apr. 19	Mishima Kimiyo	Sakura Gallery / Aichi
1985	Mar. 1—Mar. 24	Mishima Kimiyo	Gallery Ueda-Warehouse / Tokyo
1988	Sep. 27—Oct. 9	Mishima Kimiyo Exhibition	galerie 16 / Kyoto
1989	Jul. 24—Aug. 5	Mishima Kimiyo: Fossilized Information	Muramatsu Gallery / Tokyo
1990	Nov. 5—Nov. 7	MISHIMA KIMIYO	Galerie Pousse / Tokyo
	Sep. 3—Sep. 28	Mishima Kimiyo: Clay Crazy	INAX Gallery 2 / Tokyo, INAX Gallery / Osaka
1992	Nov. 2—Nov. 21	Mishima Kimiyo	Kasahara Gallery / Osaka
1994	Mar. 14—Mar. 24	Mishima Kimiyo Works from the Collection	Galerie Pousse / Tokyo
1998	Apr. 7—Apr. 19	Mishima Kimiyo	Art Front Gallery / Tokyo Hill Side Galley / Tokyo
1999	Sep. 1—Sep. 28	Mishima Kimiyo: Crazy Paper	INAX Gallery 2 / Tokyo
2001			K. Mikimoto & Co., Ltd. / Tokyo
	Sep. 25—Oct. 19	Mishima Kimiyo: The Debris of Information (Memories of the 20th Century)	Muramatsu Gallery / Tokyo
2004	Sep. 16—Oct. 12	Mishima Kimiyo: 1960s Paintings	Contemporary Art Museum ISE
	Jul. 1—Jul. 16	Mishima Kimiyo: 1960s Paintings	Gallery Nii / Osaka, Tokyo
2011	May 26—May 29	Mishima Kimiyo	Art HK 11 (Booth of MEM) / Hong Kong
2013	Nov. 9—Dec. 14	MISHIMA KIMIYO PAINTING PERIOD: 1954-1970	Gallery Yamaki Fine Art / Hyogo

2014	Nov. 29	Mishima Kimiyo Pre-opening Exhibition	ART FACTORY Jonanjima
2015	Dec. 5—Feb. 28, 2016	Mishima Kimiyo Installation [Permanent Exhibition]	ART FACTORY Jonanjima
2016	Mar. 11—Apr. 9	Mishima Kimiyo	Taka Ishii Gallery / New York
	Mar. 24—Mar. 26	Mishima Kimiyo	Art Basel Hong Kong (Booth of MEM) / Hong Kong
2017	Feb. 22—Feb. 26	Mishima Kimiyo	COSTUME NATIONAL LAB: MITSUI FINE ARTS / Tokyo
	May 2—May 28	Mishima Kimiyo	Sokyo Gallery / Kyoto
	May 5—May 7	Mishima Kimiyo	Frieze New York (Booth of Gallery Yamaki Fine Art) / New York
	Sep. 2—Sep. 30	Mishima Kimiyo	Gallery Yamaki Fine Art / Hyogo
	Oct. 7—Nov. 5	Mishima Kimiyo: Early Works	MEM / Tokyo
	Nov. 9—Nov. 12	Mishima Kimiyo	ART021 (Booth of Sokyo Gallery) / Shanghai
2018	May 18—Jun. 14	Mishima Kimiyo: Paintings	Nonaka Hill / Los Angeles
	Jun. 8—Jul. 13	MISHIMA KIMIYO: Paintings and Sculptures	Anne Mosseri-Marlio Gallery / Basel
	Sep. 1—Sep. 28	MISHIMA KIMIYO Works since the Painting Period: 1970-	Gallery Yamaki Fine Art / Hyogo
2019	Nov. 1—Nov. 3	Mishima Kimiyo	Artissima 2019 (Booth of Sokyo Gallery) / Torino
2020	Jan. 16—Jan. 19	Mishima Kimiyo	Taipei Dangdai (Booth of Sokyo Gallery) / Taipei
	Mar. 14—Jul. 5	Mishima Kimiyo	MEM / Tokyo
	Oct. 3—Oct. 31	MISHIMA KIMIYO EXHIBITION	Gallery Yamaki Fine Art / Hyogo
	Oct. 24—Dec. 12	Mishima Kimiyo	Sokyo Lisbon / Lisbon
	Dec. 24—Mar. 7, 2021	4th Collection Gallery Exhibition 2020-2021: Special Feature Mishima Kimiyo	The National Museum of Modern Art, Kyoto
2021	Jan. 27—Feb. 27	Mishima Kimiyo	Sokyo Annex / Kyoto
	Feb. 9—Mar. 21	Mishima Kimiyo	SHOP Taka Ishii Gallery / Hong Kong
	Jul. 15—Sep. 4	Mishima Kimiyo Solo Exhibition: 1950s – 2021	SOKYO ATSUMI / Tokyo
	Sep. 21—Oct. 6	Mishima Kimiyo I Papier Collé	MEM / Tokyo
2022	Jan. 29—Feb. 8, 2021	Mishima Kimiyo Exhibition	Ginza Tsutaya Books
2023	Feb. 2—Apr. 26	Mishima Kimiyo	Sokyo Gallery / Kyoto
	Sep. 16—Nov. 26	Mishima Kimiyo: Play Watch Create	Museum of Modern Ceramic Art, Gifu
2024	Feb. 15—Apr. 17	Mishima Kimiyo	Sokyo Gallery, Sokyo Annex / Kyoto
	May 19—Jul. 7	Mishima Kimiyo: Memories for the Future	Nerima Art Museum

Group Exhibitions

Year	Dates	Title	Venue
1954		Dokuritsu Exhibition (23-37th, 1955-69)	Tokyo Metropolitan Art Museum
		Kansai Dokuritsu Exhibition (1955-69)	Osaka City Museum of Fine Arts
1961		Dokuritsu Young Artists Exhibition (1962-70)	Tokyo Metropolitan Art Museum
1962		Asahi Young Artists Exhibition Osaka, Organized by The Asahi Shimbun	Takashimaya Osaka, Takashimaya Kyoto
		1st Montagne Exhibition (2nd-5th: 1963-66)	Mall Gallery / Kyoto, Osaka Gallery

1963	Oct.	Mishima Shigeji & Mishima Kimiyo	galerie 16 / Kyoto
1964	Mar. 4—Mar. 15	galerie16 Young Artists Exhibition	Miyako Hotel / Kyoto
	Apr. 4—May 10	Trends in Contemporary Japanese Painting and Sculpture	The National Museum of Modern Art, Kyoto
	Nov. 20—Nov. 27	The 3rd International Young Artists Exhibition, Europe and Japan, Organized by Japan Culture Forum	Seibu Ikebukuro SSS Hall
1965	Sep. 10—Sep. 25	The 9th Shell Art Award Exhibition	Shirokiya / Tokyo
1966		Mainichi Shimbun Art Competition	Kyoto Municipal Museum of Art
1967	Mar. 4—Mar. 14	The 4th International Young Artists Exhibition, U.S.A. and Japan, Organized by Japan Culture Forum	Seibu Ikebukuro
1968		Ibaraki Contemporary Art Exhibition	Ibaraki Civic Hall
1971		The 1st Japan Ceramic Art Exhibition, Avant-garde Section, organized by The Mainichi Newspaper Co., Ltd. [touring to North America] (2nd-5th, 1973, [touring to Central and South America], 1975, 1977, 1979)	Daimaru Department Store Okayama Prefecture General Culture Center toured to USA and Canada
1972		International Competition of Contemporary Ceramic Art in Faenza	The International Museum of Ceramics in Faenza
	Jun. 6—Jun. 11	10th Year Exhibition	galerie16 / Kyoto
	Oct. 19—Oct. 21	The 1st Ashiyagawa International Biennale	Luna Hall / Hyogo
1973		International Ceramics	Calgary*
		Chunichi International Exhibition of Ceramic Art, organized by The Chunichi Shimbun	Nagoya Mitsukoshi Department Store
	Aug. 18—Oct. 14	International Cup Exhibition, organized by The Hokkoku Shimbun	Museum of Art of Exposition Sea of Japan
1974		The 2nd Ashiyagawa International Biennale	Tekisui Museum of Art / Hyogo
	May 10—May 30	The 11th International Art Exhibition, organized by The Mainichi Shimbun	Tokyo Metropolitan Art Museum Kyoto Municipal Museum of Art
1975		The Exhibition of Modern Japanese Prints	The Museum of Modern Art, Ferrara
	Jan. 5—Jan. 19	Art Now '75	Hyogo Prefectural Museum of Modern Art
	Jan. 18—Feb. 2	Quarter of a Century of Contemporary Art	Tokyo Central Museum
	May 10—May 30	The 11th Contemporary Art Exhibition of Japan	Tokyo Metropolitan Art Museum Kyoto Municipal Museum of Art
	Sep. 24—Sep. 30	The 8th Contemporary Exhibition	Daimaru Department Store / Kyoto
1976		The 11th Japan Art Festival	The Ueno Royal Museum Washington State University
		International Print Biennale in Krakow	The National Museum in Krakow
		Contemporary Japanese Ceramics	Touring Australia* and New Zealand*
		Contemporary Art Exhibition of Japan, organized by The Mainichi Shimbun	Tokyo Metropolitan Art Museum
	Jun. 13—Sep. 12	The 5th British International Print Biennale (the 6th: 1979)	Cartwright Hall / Bradford
	Sep. 1—Oct. 31	Modern and Traditional Ceramics from Japan	The Rostock Art Gallery The Staatliche Kunstammlungen Dresden
1977	Apr. 22—Apr. 27	The 1st Contemporary Japanese Art Print Grand Prix Exhibition	Ginza Matsuya Department Store

1978		Ceramic New Map Centering on Osaka	Osaka Municipal Gallery
	Jun. 3—Jun. 28	An Exhibition of Women Artists from Japan	A.I.R. Gallery, New York
	Aug. 24—Sep. 17	Contemporary Japanese Crafts	The National Museum of Modern Art, Kyoto
	Sep. 12—Sep. 17	Contemporary Craftsmen	Kyoto Municipal Museum of Art
1979	Apr. 14—May 20	Contemporary Crafts: form the collection of The National Museum of Modern Art, Kyoto	The Museum of Modern Art, Gunma
	Apr. 21—Jun. 10	Japanese Ceramics Today: from the Kyoto National Museum of Modern Arto	Denver Art Museum
	Aug. 8—Aug. 20	Shimizu Kusuo and Artists	Minami Gallery / Tokyo
1980	Jul. —Sep.	The 7th International Biennale of Contemporary Ceramics	Magnelli Museum – Museum of Ceramics / Vallauris
	May 24—Jul. 13	International Exhibition of Playful Pottery	Hokkaido Museum of Modern Art
	Jul. 25—Sep. 23	Simulated Landscape in Contemporary Art	The National Museum of Art, Osaka
	Oct. 25—Nov. 10	Claywork: From Traditional To Avangarde (1981)	Otsu Seibu Department Store Ikebukuro Seibu Department Store
	Oct. 26—Nov. 23	Prints of Japan 1985	Tochigi Prefectural Museum of Fine Arts
1981		Contemporary Japan and China Ceramics	National Museum of Taiwan History / Taipei
		The World of Play: Another Design	Osaka Design Center
	Mar. 7—Mar. 29	Art Now: 1970-1980	Hyogo Prefectural Museum of Modern Art
	Nov. 1—Nov. 7	Caricature and Humour: Today's Ema Tablet Exhibition	Station Building Kawasaki
1982		Contemporary Japanese Ceramics	Faenza*, Roma*, National Museum of Fine Arts of Quebec, Hong Kong Museum of Art
	Feb. 11—Feb. 23	Art in Daily Life Exhibition	Tobu Department Store Communication Space
	Apr. 17—May 9	Clay Work Now I, What Can Be Done With Clay And Fire '82 Yamaguchi	Yamaguchi Prefectural Art Museum
	Apr. 27—May 5	Visual Circus, touring around Japan	Ginza Matsuya Department Store Shizuoka Isetan Department Store Takashimaya Yokohama Department Store toured to other venues
	Sep. 7—Sep. 12	The 3th International Impact Art Festival '82 (The 4th: 1983 [toured to Soul])	Kyoto Municipal Museum of Art
1983		Kijo no New York Exhibition	Seibu Engine Room, Tokyo
		Specimen Box Exhibition: Specimen of the Times	Sony Building / Tokyo
		Artists' International Book Exhibition 1983	Miyazaki Gallery / Osaka
		The Exhibition of Miniatures 14X14	Arc Building / Kyoto San Francisco Museum of Modern Art
	Jun. 29—Sep. 25	A Look at Today's Contemporary Japanese Art	Museum of Modern Art and History, Geneve
	Oct. 4—Dec. 4	Contemporary Realism	The Museum of Modern Art, Saitama
1984		Exhibition: Ceramics × 27	Gallery Kiállitás / Budapest
		Collection of Play	Gallery Ueda / Tokyo
		Japanese Contemporary Ceramics	Maya Behn Gallery / Zurich
		Ceramics Today (1985)	Seibu Department Store
1985		Kitsch	Ban Gallery, Osaka

		Exhibition of 120 Contemporary Ceramic Artists, Organized by Kodansha co., Ltd.	Chinzanso / Tokyo, toured to other venues
		Book Shelf Sculpture	galerie16 / Kyoto
		Artists' Books: Japan	Franklin Furnace / New York Fuji Television Gallery / Tokyo
		KIS'85 Kunsan International Show	Kunsan National University Museum
	Apr. 20	Yamamura Collection Exhibition	The National Museum of Art, Osaka
	May 13—May 25	International Art Book Exhibition	Miyazaki Gallery / Osaka
	Jul. 13—Aug. 4	10 Spiez Ceramics Exhibition	Spiez*
	Aug. 16—Aug. 28	World Humour Cup Exhibition: Playful Pottery	Odakyu Deapartment Store / Tokyo
	Sep. 2—Sep. 14	Osaka Contemporary Art Fair 1985	Contemporary Art Center / Osaka
	Sep. 7—Sep. 21	Invited to Contemporary Ceramic Arts Exhibition	Gallery Isogaya / Tokyo
	Oct. 5—Nov. 4	Toward the Museum of Tommorow II, Image as Environment	Hyogo Prefectural Museum of Modern Art
	Oct. 21—Nov. 12	Charity Exhibition for Africa	Gallery Isogaya / Tokyo
	Dec. 7—Jan. 26, 1986	Prints of Japan 1985	Tochigi Prefectural Museum of Fine Arts
1986		Ceramic Now	Seibu Gallery / Tokyo
		Clay Work '86: Pouring Images	Gallery Maronie / Kyoto
		Reading Objects: Literature and Objects	Gallery Iteza / Kyoto
		Contemporary Ceramics	Budapest*
	Jan. 2—Jan. 26	Clay: Image and Sphere 1981-85	Seibu Hall / Otsu, Yurakucho Art Forum
	May 9—Jul. 4	Contemporary Japanese Ceramics	Everson Museum of Art / Syracuse
	Jun. 23—Jun. 29	ESTIU Japan '86	Museu de la Garrotxa / Olot
	Jul. 29—Sep. 21	The Collection Exhibition, Mid-term Japanese Prints	Tokyo Metropolitan Art Museum
1987	Jan. 6—Feb. 11	Clay and Fire Exhibition: Creative Development and Potentials	The Museum of Fine Art, Gifu
	Mar. 6—Mar. 27	The World of Print 2: Silkscreen Printing	Hokkaido Museum of Modern Art
	May 9—May 27	Object: Deviated Matter	Seibu Tsukashin Hall / Hyogo
1988		Coffee Cup in Europe	Brussels*
		Two Person Exhibition with Seiji Kunishima	Hankyu Department Store, Los Angeles
		Drawing Exhibition	Gallery Cuore / Osaka
	Jul. —Aug.	The 9th Biennale International Limoges	Limoges*
	Sep. 2—Sep. 13	Art Viewed with Hands	Yurakucho Art Forum Art Forum / Tokyo Tsukasin Hall / Hyogo Oita Prefecture Museum of Art
	Sep. 10—Oct. 9	East-West Contemporary Ceramic Exhibition: Olympic Art Festival	Arts Council Korea
	Sep. 15—Sep. 30	The 2nd Ceramic Art '88 Toki, Japan	Tokishi Bunka Plaza / Toki
1989		Exhibiton from the New Acquisition Collection	Tochigi Prefectural Museum of Fine Arts
	Feb. 2—Mar. 25	Development of Contemporary Art from the Museum Collection	Tokyo Metropolitan Art Museum
	Feb. 20—Feb. 25	Claimed Objects Exhibition '89	Shinanobashi Gallery / Osaka

Year	Date	Exhibition	Venue
	Mar. 4—Mar. 23	Illusion of Yamamura Collection	Hyogo Prefectural Museum of Modern Art
	Jun. 17—Jul. 23	Art Exciting 89: Beyond the Present	The Museum of Modern Art, Saitama Queensland Art Gallery / South Brisbane
	Jul. 11—Jul. 23	Back and Forth: Collage in the 1960's of Takahashi Motonao and Mishima Kimiyo	galerie 16 / Kyoto
	Oct. 1—Oct. 29	Artist in Kyoto: Yesterday. Today, Tomorrow	Kyoto Munisipal Museum of Art
	Oct. 22—Nov. 5	The 2nd International Ceramics Competition Mino '89	Tajimi
1990	Jul. 29—Sep. 16	Japanese Clay Work Today	Tochigi Prefectural Museum of Fine Arts
	Oct. 5—Dec. 1	Aspects of Contemporary Clay Art	Tokyo Metropolitan Art Museum
	Oct. 6—Oct. 28	Contemporary Ceramic 1980-1990	The Museum of Modern Art, Wakayama
1990	May 11 —May 16	Asahi Modern Craft Exhibition (1992, 1997)	Hankyu Yurakucho Department Store Hankyu Umeda Main Store
1991	Apr. 20—May 26	Metamorphosis: International Contemporary Ceramics	The Shigaraki Ceramic Cultural Park, Shiga
	Aug. 10—Oct. 6	Art Scene 1991: Each Material, Each Expression	The Tokushima Modern Art Museum
1992		Contemporary Japanese Ceramic	Everson Museum of Art / Syracuse
		International Ceramic Exhibition 1992	National Museum of Taiwan History /Taipei
	Jun. 2—Jun. 7	Kyoto Select Art Exhibition	Kyoto Municipal Museum of Art
	Aug. 5—Aug. 30	Children and Form: Children's View of Contemporary Art	Ashiya City Museum of Art and History / Hyogo
	Sep. 16—Sep. 30	Kasahara Gallery: The 20th Anniversary Exhibition	Kasahara Gallery
1993		Vision, Illusion and Anti-illusion from the Museum Collection	Tokyo Metropolitan Art Museum
	Mar. 2—Apr. 18	The 30th Anniversary of the National Museum of Modern Art, Kyoto: Crafts of the World	The National Museum of Modern Art, Kyoto
	Jul. 16—Aug. 22	Contemporary Ceramics 1950-1990	Aichi Prefectural Museum of Art
	Aug. 27—Sep. 23	Selected Works from the Collection, The 60th Anniversary Exhibition	Kyoto Municipal Museum of Art
	Oct. 2—Dec. 5	Utsuwa: Always Looking at Life from an Angle	The Museum of Modern Art, Saitama
	Dec. 12—Mar. 21, 1994	Repetition and Multiplication in Contemporary Art from the Museum Collection	Tokyo Metropolitan Art Museum
1994	Feb. 8—Mar. 27	Japanese Art of the 1960s-1970s from the Museum Collection	Tokyo Metropolitan Art Mueum
1995		The International Exhibition of Contemporary Ceramics	The Shigaraki Ceramic Cultural Park The Museum of Contemporary Ceramic Art
		Wind of Faenza: Japanese Winner	Ceratopia Toki
		Magical Viewpoint	Hirakata City Gotenyama Art Center
	Apr. 19—Jun. 4	Japanese Culture of the Fifty Postwar Years 1945-1995	Meguro Museum of Art, Tokyo Hiroshima City Museum of Contemporary Art Hyogo Prefectural Museum of Modern Art Fukuoka Prefectural Museum of Art
1996		Sai no Kuni Saitama, Sculpture Variety '96 (1998)	Okegawa Station West Park
	Apr. 20—Jul. 7	Aspects of Japanese Ceramic Art	The Hakone Open-Art Museum
	Nov. 23—Dec. 27	Cross Section of the Post War Period Art; From the Yamamura Collection of Hyogo Prefectural Museum of Modern Art	Chiba City Museum of Art

Year	Date	Exhibition	Venue
1997	Feb. 1—Mar. 24	Yamamura Collection: Contemporary Art Viewed by a Collector	Hyogo Prefectural Museum of Modern Art
	Mar. —Mar., 1998	Permanent Collection: 50 Years of Contemporary Art	Museum of Contemporary Art Tokyo
1998		The Hope II	Safa Gallery / Budapest Hungarian Museum of Photography / Kecskemét
	Sep. 24—Nov. 15	Itinerant International Exhibition, Japan-Brazil 98-99	The São Paulo Museum of Art Rio de Janeiro Museum of Modern Art
1999		The Plate Exhibition	Collins Gallery of University of Strathclyde / London
	Feb. 16—Mar. 28	Post War Period Art Kansai 1950s-1990s	The Museum of Modern Art, Wakayama
	Oct. 8—Dec. 12	Collection in Focus: What You See Is What You Get, or Is It?	Museum of Contemporary Art Tokyo
2000		The International Ceramic Exhibition	Keramion* / Frechen
2001	Jul. 12—Nov. 11	The 19th Exhibition of Contemporary Japanese Sculpture	Ube City Outdoor Sculpture Museum
2002		Imaging the Book, Exhibition of Contemporary Art	The Royal Library of Alexandria
	Jul. 20—Sep. 1	Metamorphosis: Introduction to Art for Children and Grown-ups	The Museum of Modern Art, Gunma
	Oct. 12—Jan. 19, 2003	The Legacy of Modern Ceramic Art: Part1 From Artisan to Artist, The Evolution of Japanese Ceramic Art	Museum of Modern Ceramic Art, Gifu
	Oct. 20—Nov. 04	The 3rd Japan Humorous Pottery Sculpture Exhibition Ceratopia Toki, Gifu	
2003	Oct. 9—Nov. 25	The Art of Earth: Clay Works of the New Century	The National Museum of Art, Osaka
	Jul. 11—Sep. 21	Trace of a Company Employee's Art Collection: A Place for Post-War Japanese Art	Shunan City Museum of Art and History Mitaka City Gallery of Art Fukui City Art Museum
2004	May 24—Jun. 29	Contemporary Codex: Ceramics and Book	University Art Gallery of Central Michigan University / Mt. Plesant, toured to other venues in USA
2005		Japanese Art, World Art: 50 Years	Museum of Contemporary Art Tokyo
	Jan. 13—Apr. 10	My Landscape	Ikeda Museum of 20th Century Art
	Apr. 16—Jun. 19	Art as Riddle	Hamada Children's Museum of Art
	Jun. 19—Sep. 25	Contemporary Ceramics in Japan and Abroad - An Era of Power	The Shigaraki Ceramic Cultural Park, The Museum of Contemporary Ceramic Art
	Jul. 24—Sep. 11	Japanese Women Artist in Avant-garde Movements, 1950-1975	Tochigi Prefectural Museum of Fine Arts
	Oct. 7—Jul. 9, 2006	Contemporary Clay: Japanese Ceramics for the New Century	Museum of Fine Arts, Boston, toured to other venues in New York
2006	Jan. 21—Mar. 21	The Quintessence of Modern Japanese Ceramics	Ibaraki Ceramic Art Museum
	Apr. 25—Aug. 13	Japan Real: Each Reality in Ceramics	Museum of Modern Ceramic Art, Gifu
	Nov. 17—Feb. 26, 2007	Avant-garde and Tradition of the Japanese Ceramics	Musée National de Céramique, Sèvres
2007		Hermandades Escultóricas Mexico-Japan 2007	Merida* / Yucatán
	May 25—Jul. 1	Depicting Words in Art, Masterpieces from the Permanent Collection 1	Kyoto Municipal Museum of Art
	Jun. 10—Sep. 24	Soaring Voices: Contemporary Japanese Women Ceramic Artists (–2012)	The Shigaraki Ceramic Cultural Park The Museum of Contemporary Ceramic Art Shiga The New Otani Museum / Tokyo Shizuoka Art Gallery, toured to other venues in USA

	Nov. 8—Dec. 15	Breaking the Mold	Galley Joan Mirviss / New York
	Dec. 23—Mar. 28, 2008	Various Aspects of Avant-garde Ceramic Art	Museum of Modern Ceramic Art, Gifu
2008	Mar. 1—Mar. 20	Osaka Art Kaleidoscope 2008: Osaka Time	Osaka Contemporary Art Center
2009	Aug. 22—Sep. 23	World of Trick Art (–2011)	Toyohashi City Museum of Art and History Takamatsu Art Museum, toured to other venues
2010	Apr. —Dec.	OAP Sculpture Path 2010 UN-SYNTAX	ARTCOURT Gallery / Osaka
	Nov. 2—Dec. 5	The Newspapers	Kanda Nissho Memorial Museum of Art, Hokkaido
	Nov. 20—Jan. 23, 2011	This Is Not a Book: Spreading of Book Art	Urawa Art Museum Fukui City Art Museum
2011	Sep. 2—Sep. 23	Living Ceramics: The Japanese Ceramists awarded of Faenza	Italian Institute of Culture Tokyo Gallery Voice, Tajimi
2012	Mar. 3—Jul. 6	The Magic of Ceramics: Artistic Inspiration (-2013)	The Shigaraki Ceramic Cultural Park, The Museum of Contemporary Ceramic Art, Shiga Museum of Ceramic Art, Hyogo Museum of Modern Ceramic Art, Gifu
	Apr. 21—Jun. 27	The Japan Foundation Collection: The Japanese Modern Ceramics Go around the World	Ibaraki Ceramic Art Museum
	Apr. 21—Aug. 19	2012 Spring Exhibition: POP/ Bring to Life	Museum of Modern Ceramic Art, Gifu
	Aug. 22—Sep. 22	The Link between Words and Art: An Homage to Nakahara Yusuke	Gallery Yamaki Fine Art, Kobe
2013	Dec. 21—Feb. 11, 2014	Materials and Substance(s)	The Museum of Modern Art, Wakayama
2014	May 9—May 28	Currents: Japanese Contemporary Art	Christie's, Hong Kong
	Jul. 5—Aug. 24	Identity and Originality	The Museum of Ceramic Art, Hyogo
	Aug. 1—Sep. 15	Wow! Exciting Art & Craft	Urasoe Art Museum
2015	Jan. 17—Apr. 4	Ancient to Modern: Japanese Contemporary Ceramics and their Sources	San Antonio Museum of Art
	Jun. 13—Aug. 30	Cute Curious Ceramics	Museum of Modern Ceramic Art, Gifu
2016	Jan. 25—Feb. 21	Chronicle, Chronicle!	Creative Center Osaka
2017	Feb. 4—Mar. 26	The 30th Anniversary Exhibition: Selection of Letter and Signal	Hakodate Museum of Modern Art, Hokkaido
	Mar. 21—Nov. 25, 2018	Show Me the Mini	Samuel P. Harn Museum of ArtUniversity of Florida
	Apr. 18—Jun. 18	Collection x Chronicle	Museum of Modern Ceramic Art, Gifu
	Apr. 24—May 31	Gyeonggi World Ceramic Biennale 2017, Narrative, Ode to Life, Cerapia	Icheon Cerapia, Gyeonggi-do / Icheon
	Jun. 9—Jul. 29	Painting on the Edge: A Historical Survey	Stephen Friedman Gallery, London
	Jul. 15—Sep. 18	2D Printers	Tochigi Prefectural Museum of Fine Arts
2018	Jan. 13—Mar. 10	The Superlative Artistry of Japan	The Japan Cultural Institute in Cologne, toured to other cities
	Mar. 24—Apr. 15	Mishima Shigeji and Mishima Kimiyo	MEM / Tokyo
	Nov. 3—Jan. 20, 2019	Collection 2: The 1980s Zeitgeist as a Point of Departure	The National Museum of Art, Osaka
2019	Mar. 29—Jun. 16	Weavers of Worlds - A Century of Flux in Japanese Modern/Contemporary Art	Museum of Contemporary Art Tokyo

	Aug. 3—Sep. 29	Yamamura Collection: Gutai and the Japanese Avant-garde 1950s-1980s	Hyogo Prefectural Museum of Art
	Sep. 1—Sep. 8	CONTACT: Where the World Meets Japanese Art and Culture	Kiyomizu temple, Kyoto
2020	Feb. 6—Nov. 20	Psychic Wounds: On Art & Trauma	The Warehouse / Dallas
	Sep. 5—Oct. 4	On Mono, Koto and Body - Six Perspectives	MEM / Tokyo
	Sep. 19—Nov. 8	Ashiya Time: A Large Collection Exhibition	Ashiya City Museum of Art and History
2021	Apr. 22—Jan. 16, 2022	Another Energy: Power to Continue Challenging -16 Women Artists from around the World	Mori Art Museum / Tokyo
	May 9—Jul. 4	The Floating Bridge: Postmodern and Contemporary Japanese Ceramics	Everson Museum of Art, Syracuse
	Jun. 15—Jul. 4	SPUR by MEM	MEM / Tokyo
	Oct. 15—Feb. 6, 2022	The Flames: The Age of Ceramics	The Museum of Modern Art, Paris
	Nov. 13—Feb. 23, 2022	MOT Collection: Journals Vol.2	Museum of Contemporary Art Tokyo
	Dec. 4—Apr. 25, 2022	The 10th Asia Pacific Triennial of Contemporary Art	Queensland Art Gallery
2022	Feb. 5—Mar. 27	Gifts from the 20th Century: The Pleasure of Appreciating Modern and Contemporary Art	The Museum of Modern Art, Wakayama
	Apr. 9—Sep. 6	From Monet to Richter: Focus on New Acquisitions –Pola Museum of Art 20th Anniversary Exhibition	Pola Museum of Art / Kanagawa
	Apr. 16—May 14	Gyfa Show II Post-War Female Artists 1970–2017	Gallery Yamaki Fine Art / Hyogo
	Apr. 20—Aug. 28	Body and Writing: Today's Art from New Acquisition of Museum of Modern Art, Paris	The city of Paris Museum of Modern Art
	Aug. 15—Sep. 25	Void of Nippon 77: Landscape and Repetition in Postwar Art	GYRE gallery / Tokyo
	Nov. 14—Nov. 19	Fiscal Year 2021's Japan Ceramics Association Gold Award Prize: Kuwata Takuro and Mishima Kimiyo	Kocyukyo / Tokyo
	Nov. 23—Jan. 29, 2023	Permanent Exhibition	Contemporary Art Museum ISE
2023	Jan. 20—Mar. 5	11th Enku Grand Award Exhibition: Resonances -Transmission and Creation in the Spirit of Enku-	The Museum of Fine Arts, Gifu
	Apr. 28—Jul. 2	Re: Startline 1963-1970/2023 Sympathetic Relations between the Museum and Artists as Seen in the Trends in Contemporary Japanese Art Exhibition	The National Museum of Modern Art, Kyoto
	May 23—Sep. 10	MOMAT Collection	The National Museum of Modern Art, Tokyo
	Jun. 13—Jul. 2	The Great Wall 1963-1970: The Artist's Style at the Time of the Gallery's Opening	galerie16 / Kyoto
	Sep. 30—Feb. 25, 2024	TAKEUCHI COLLECTION: The Lens within Your Heart	WHAT MUSEUM／Tokyo
	Dec. 16—Jan. 3, 2024	Radical Clay: Contemporary Women Artists from Japan	The Art Institute of Chicago

参考資料
Reference Data

【凡例】
・所収論文は各文献の末尾に（　）内で記した。
・新聞の地方版の表記は省略した。

個展

『三島喜美代展』村松画廊、1972年（乾由明「三島喜美代のやきもの」）
『三島喜美代展』南画廊、1974年（乾由明「やきものとしての印刷物—三島喜美代の作品について」）
『三島喜美代展』ギャラリー上田、1985年（中原佑介「三島喜美代の新作」）
『三島喜美代展—化石になった情報』村松画廊、1989年
『Painting Period 1954-1970』ギャラリーヤマキファインアート、2013年
『三島喜美代—installation works 1984-2014』美術資料センター株式会社、2015年（建畠晢「三島喜美代へのオマージュ」7-9頁）
『三島喜美代—installation works 1984-2014』美術資料センター株式会社、2015年（秋元雄史「圧倒的な存在感を放つゴミたち—三島喜美代の美」13-16頁）
『三島喜美代』美術資料センター株式会社、2015年（河崎晃一「三島喜美代のコラージュの時代」6-7頁）
『KIMIYO MISHIMA—Fossils of Information』MEM、2016年
『三島喜美代—Early Works』MEM、2017年
『Mishima Kimiyo』艸居、2017年、4-5頁（秋元雄史「さて、三島喜美代さんのことについて話そう。」）
『三島喜美代』ギャラリーヤマキファインアート、2017年（飯尾由貴子「つくりつづける—三島喜美代が見つめるもの」）
『KIMIYO MISHIMA—Works since the painting period: 1970-』ギャラリーヤマキファインアート、2018年
『三島喜美代展』ギャラリーヤマキファインアート、2020年（飯尾由貴子「裏も表も三島喜美代」）
『三島喜美代』MEM、2020年、6-7頁
『三島喜美代—Mishima Kimiyo』艸居、2021年（「三島喜美代は語る—ハンス・ウルリッヒ・オブリスト」73-137頁）
『三島喜美代—遊ぶ 見つめる 創りだす』岐阜県現代陶芸美術館、2023年（建畠晢「三島喜美代の独自性について」6-8頁／榎本徹「光景へのコラージュ—三島喜美代の作品世界」12-13頁／花井素子「三島喜美代—遊ぶ 見つめる 創りだす」97-99頁／「三島喜美代インタビュー—2023年7月19日 大阪・十三のアトリエにて」103-105頁）

グループ展

『独立展出品目録』（第22-37回）独立美術協会、1954-69年
『女性作家招待展・日本』A.I.R画廊、1978年
『現代の陶芸1—いま、土と火でなにが可能か』山口県立美術館、1983年（榎本徹「展覧会ノート—いま、土と火でなにが可能か」）
『土・イメージと形体』西武美術館、1986年（乾由明「クレイワーク—そのモダンとポストモダン」）
『土と炎展—新たな展開と可能性』岐阜県立美術館、1987年（乾由明「現代における土と炎の造形」）
上田カルチャープロジェクツ 編『GALLEY UEDA WAREHOUSE』ギャラリー上田ウエアハウス、1987年
『オブジェ—逸脱する物質』つかしんホール、1987年（「三島喜美代」40-41頁）
『手で見る美術展』西武美術館、1988年（三島喜美代「やきものになった印刷物」80頁）
『BACK AND FORTH COLLAGE IN THE 1960's』ギャラリー16、1989年（中西至宏「テキスト」）
『京都の美術 昨日・きょう・明日 III—新規収蔵品と珠玉の名品』京都市美術館、1989年（三島喜美代「陶になった印刷物」）
『現代の土』展、東京都美術館、1990年（乙葉哲「現代美術における土の造形」7-10頁）
『現代の土』展、東京都美術館、1990年（三島喜美代「"土"は私にとって」24頁）
和歌山県立美術館 編『現代の陶芸—1980-1990展』白光印刷有限会社、1990年（三島喜美代「やきものの情報」72頁）
平山郁、金子百合子 編『現代陶芸うつわ考—視線はいつも暮らしの角度で』埼玉県立近代美術館、1993年、155頁
『開催記念展1 現代陶芸の100年展—第1部 日本陶芸の展開』岐阜県現代陶芸美術館、2002年、138頁
『第3回 日本ユーモア陶彫展'02』セラトピア土岐 美術ギャラリー、2002年
周南市美術博物館、赤松裕樹 編『あるサラリーマン・コレクションの軌跡—戦後日本美術の場所』あるサラリーマン・コレクションの軌跡展実行委員会、2003年、125頁
安來正博、鎌田智子 編『大地の芸術ークレイワーク新世紀』国立国際美術館、2003年（安來正博「三島喜美代」97-98頁）
Museum of Fine Arts, Boston, North Halsey, North Alice (eds.), *Contemporary clay: Japanese ceramics for the new century*, MFA Publications: Boston, 2005
小勝禮子、由本みどり 編『前衛の女性—1950-1975』栃木県立美術館、2005年
『日本陶芸100年の精華—茨城県陶芸美術館開館5周年記念』茨城県陶芸美術館、2006年

『大阪時間—大阪アート・カレイドスコープ2008』大阪府立現代美術センター、2008年(小吹隆文「アトリエ訪問記—三島喜美代インタビュー」12-13頁)
『陶芸の魅力×アートのドキドキ』滋賀県立陶芸の森、2012年、94-97頁
『独立美術協会80年史』独立美術協会80年史編集委員会、2012年
Show Me The Mini, Samuel P. Harn Museum of Art, 2017
The Japan Foundation, *The Superlative Artistry of Japan*, 2018 (Ryuichi Matsubara, "Kimiyo Mishima", p.56)
山本和弘 編『2Dプリンターズ—芸術 世界の承認をめぐる闘争について』栃木県立美術館、2017年、52-53頁
Mark Gomes, Stephanie Kennard, Zenobia Frost, *The 10 Asia Pacific Triennial of Contemporary Art*, Queensland Art Gallery, 2021
『アナザーエナジー展—挑戦しつづける力ー世界の女性アーティスト16人』森美術館 編、フィルムアート社、2021年(建畠哲「大いなる逸脱の力学」257-258頁/片岡真実「アナザーエナジー ステレオタイプ、カテゴリー、完璧さから自由であるために」280-290頁/マーティン・ゲルマン「アナザーエナジー 未来のための16人のアーティストたち」280-290頁)
『MOTコレクション Journals 日々、記す vol.2』東京都現代美術館、2021年(水田有子「三島喜美代、郭徳俊」18-21頁)
『ポーラ美術館開館20周年記念展 モネからリヒターへ—新収蔵作品を中心に』公益財団法人ポーラ美術振興財団ポーラ美術館、2022年(工藤弘二「第17章 三島喜美代—時代を表現する」184-189頁)
『第11回円空大賞展』岐阜県美術館、2023年
牧口千夏 編『Re: スタートライン—1963-1970/2023 現代美術の動向展シリーズにみる美術館とアーティストの共感関係』京都国立近代美術館、2023年

単行本

乾由明『現代日本の陶芸』(第16巻)講談社、1977年、111-115頁/137-199頁
『現代日本の陶芸—明日の造形を求めて』(第15巻)講談社、1985年(鈴木健二「やきものと印刷の出会い」36-41頁、135-136頁/三島喜美代「やきものになった印刷物」137頁)
三島喜美代『陶 vol.12 三島喜美代』京都書院、1992年(井上明彦「序」2頁)
関直子 編『東京都現代美術館の女性作家たち』(東京都現代美術館叢書3)東京都現代美術館、1997年
本間正義『美術家五十人のポートレート+α』本間正義、2001年、30-31頁
Judith S. Schwartz, *Confrontational Ceramics*, University of Pennsylvania Press, 2008
『日本列島「現代アート」を旅する』小学館、2015年(秋元雄史「ゴミを擬人化したアート」80-101頁)〔再掲:『日本で見られる現代アート傑作11』小学館、2022年(秋元雄史「ゴミを擬態化したアート」75-96頁)〕
『アート鑑賞BOOK』三笠書房、2017年(三井一弘「陶土に込めた『現代社会の危機』—三島喜美代」125-128頁)
芥川喜好『時の余白に 続』みすず書房、2018年、228-231頁
中塚宏行『美術/漂流—学芸員Nの軌跡』(第3巻)、2021年、190-193頁
『大原美術館 + 作品151と建築』大原美術館、2022年(長谷川祐里「三島喜美代」136頁)
Bert Winther-Tamaki, TSUCHI, *Earthy Materials in Contemporary Japanese Art*, University of Minnesota Press, 2022
Alice North, Halsey North and Louise Allison Cort, et al., *Listening to clay : conversations with contemporary Japanese ceramic artists*, The Monacelli Press, 2022

定期刊行物(雑誌)

『朝日ジャーナル』8号、1966年3月6日、表紙
日高てる「個展評(関西)」『日本美術』69号、1970年7月、71-72頁
神代雄一郎「日本陶芸展の混乱—日本陶芸が現代芸術になるとき」『藝術新潮』7月号、1971年7月、64-71頁
「現代陶芸の世界」『自然と盆栽—古陶歳時記』24号、1972年3月、42-47頁
三島喜美代「注目される陶芸界の新風」『週刊朝日』2805号、1972年8月、117頁
高橋亨「一展一作」『日本美術工芸』409号、1972年10月、35頁
吉田耕三「現代日本陶芸の全貌を一同に 第2回日本陶芸展を審査して」『日本美術』99号、1973年2月、28-30頁
「第2回日本陶芸展」『日本美術』99号、1973年2月、27頁
中原佑介「コップ百変化 金沢で開かれた世界のカップ展」『芸術新潮』286号、1973年10月、110-113頁
三島喜美代「若い焼きものシリーズ⑤」『いけ花龍生』163号、1973年11月、36-38頁
「版画?陶器?彫刻?」『芸術生活』297号、1974年5月、48頁
米倉守「生活空間へ」『季刊現代彫刻』6号、1974年7月、70-71頁
鈴木健二「現代陶芸の解剖② 記号」『日本美術工芸』433号、1974年10月、68-74頁
「現代工芸」『近代の美術』30号、1975年9月
「陶によるオブジェ〈やきものとしての印刷物〉」『Viewかんざき』14号、1976年4月、12頁
三島喜美代「メモより」『日本美術』129号、1976年5月、44-45頁

乾由明「この菓子・この器94—『夏木立』と『転写模様の皿』」『アサヒグラフ』1977年8月19日、14頁
那賀裕子＋貞彦「関西—三島喜美代作品展」『美術手帖』32巻、1980年4月、262-263頁
「まがいものの光景「現代美術とユーモア」展」『アートビジョン』10巻7号、1980年9月、81頁
里中英人「やきものになった印刷物あるいは割れる新聞紙の作家 三島喜美代」『月刊陶』1巻3号、1980年10月、89-97頁
三島喜美代「転写による陶の加飾」『美術手帖｜陶芸 土と火』33巻 増刊、1981年4月、147-149頁
乾由明「生命の刻印「現代の陶芸Ⅰ—いま、土と火でなにが可能か」展を見て」『月刊陶』24号、1982年7月、20-21頁
榎本徹「七人のプロフィール」『月刊陶』24号、1982年7月、24頁
「オリジナルギャラリー エッ、ほん陶!?」『ビックコミックオリジナル』230号、1982年7月5日、140-141頁
「STARDUST—胴まわり三メートルの柱を焼いた三島喜美代」『芸術新潮』1985年4月、86頁
田中幸人「展覧会—三島喜美代 巨大化の意味するもの」『美術手帖』37巻、1985年5月、178-183頁
武井邦彦「ART REVIEW—展評東京」『三彩』452巻、1985年5月、108-109頁
吉村良夫「余次元から」『日本美術工芸』568号、1986年1月、77頁
河合晴生「収蔵作品から」『(東京都)美術館ニュース』410号、1989年2月、1頁
「三島喜美代展 閉じ込められた化石になった情報」『新美術新聞』542号、1989年7月、204-206頁
横山勝彦「REVIEWS—三島喜美代＋清水伸＋森亮太＋大森裕美子＋平木美鶴」『美術手帖』41巻、1989年10月、204-206頁
藍龍「ART REVIEW—展評東京」『三彩』505巻、1989年10月、120-121頁
平野重光「野村耕、三島喜美代の二人展」『京都市美術館ニュース』160号、1989年12月、3-4頁
中原佑介「三島喜美代の新作」『INAX ART NEWS—三島喜美代展 クレイ・クレイジー』98号、1990年、2頁
三島喜美代「固められた情報」『INAX ART NEWS—三島喜美代展 クレイ・クレイジー』98号、1990年、5頁
「三島喜美代先生とのインタビュー」『滋賀県立陶芸の森 REVIEW』10巻、1994年、8頁
入澤ユカ「みしまジック」『INAX ART NEWS—三島喜美代展 クレイ・ペーパー』201号、1999年
糸加寿美「三島喜美代」『創作市場』15号、2000年1月、6-11頁
「スポーツ姉妹都市・土岐市主催『ユーモア陶彫展』の焼津市長賞受賞作品を展示」『広報やいづ』2003年2月15日、8頁
地家光二「From our Collection 三島喜美代《NEWS PAPER F-87》」『HAKOBI NEWS』21号、2007年12月、3頁
「インタビュー三島喜美代—膨大な物量で迫る『読めない芸術』」『月刊アートコレクターズ』89号、2016年8月、30-31頁
森村泰昌「野にありて跳べ 美の活動家に会いに行く—第10回 三島喜美代」『日経回廊』10号、2016年11月、104-109頁
「今月のトップランナーvol.62 三島喜美代」『月刊アートコレクターズ』139号、2020年10月、3-6頁
Hans Ulrich Obrist, “Horror und Humor”, *Das Magazin*, Tamedia, 18 March, 2021
「THE TIME HAVE CAUGHT UP—創り続ける女性たちのエネルギー」『T JAPAN』2021年3月27日
『美感遊創—サントリーウエルネス通信』224号、2021年5月1日
小崎哲哉「アナザーエナジー展と三島喜美代」『婦人画報』1416号(7月号)、2021年6月
白坂由里「アナザーエナジー展と三島喜美代」『SPUR』(8月号)、2021年6月23日
「三島喜美代—森美術館『アナザーエナジー展』へ」『メトロポリターナトーキョー』、2021年7月10日
三島喜美代、聞き手 建畠晢、構成 杉原環樹「三島喜美代—遊ぶように制作し続ける小柄な巨人」『美術手帖』73巻、2021年8月、40-45頁
「MASTERPIECE アーティストたちのあの名作に出会う。」『Casa BRUTUS 特別編集 日本の現代アート名鑑100』マガジンハウス、2022年4月
「立体アート 超越するモノヂカラ」『月刊アートコレクターズ』162号、2022年9月、13頁、62頁
井上明彦「命がけで遊ぶ—三島喜美代さんの受賞を記念して」『陶説』833号、2022年11月、25-26頁
建畠晢「情報の化石化—日本陶磁協会賞金賞受賞記念を祝って」『陶説』833号、2022年11月、26-28頁
「日本のシルクスクリーン150年」『版画芸術』阿部出版、2022年
「報告—2021年度日本陶磁協会賞・金賞受賞記念 桑田卓郎・三島喜美代展」『陶説』835号、2023年2月、48-53頁
花井素子「特集記事—三島喜美代 遊ぶ 見つめる 創りだす」『陶説』844号、2023年11月、118-122頁

定期刊行物(新聞)

「美術 超現実を展開 爽快な現代美 異様な存在感—三島喜美代、吉本直貴、二村裕子」『朝日新聞』、1974年2月23日夕刊
「美術 趣向の変わった二つの個展 寺山修司／三島喜美代」『読売新聞』、1974年2月26日夕刊
田中幸人「三島喜美代展、ポップで風刺的な作品」『毎日新聞』、1985年3月5日
「美術 三島喜美代展、辛らつなユーモア」『読売新聞』、1985年3月22日夕刊
「美術 光の詩の輝き、消える」『朝日新聞』、1985年3月23日夕刊
「美術 一種、逆説的な写実」『朝日新聞』、1989年7月28日夕刊
「三島喜美代展」『毎日新聞』、1989年7月31日夕刊
「美術 大地が放つ死の予感—戸田成雄展、現代社会を語る廃物—三島喜美代展」『朝日新聞』、1990年9月7日夕刊
田中幸人「美術『現代の土』展、『土』の生態を視覚化」『毎日新聞』、1990年10月26日夕刊

「『美術』『やきもの』を離れ新たな土の可能性―『現代の土』展」『読売新聞』、1990年11月12日夕刊
「寸読寸見 文学における吉野時代を追い編さんなど」『日本経済新聞』、1992年6月19日夕刊
「阪神大震災 美術館活動に大打撃」『毎日新聞』、1995年2月10日夕刊
井上隆生「三島喜美代さん『壊れる』新聞創案」『朝日新聞』、1995年10月20日夕刊
三田晴夫「美術 三島喜美代展―ユーモラスな抜け殻」『毎日新聞』、1998年4月14日夕刊
宮本扶末子「三島喜美代展 クレイジー・ペーパー 来月、京橋で」『毎日新聞』、1999年8月18日
「凛・街とモニュマン 現代日本彫刻展／5 三島喜美代さん、大隅秀雄さん」『毎日新聞』、2001年8月31日
三田晴夫「美術 三島喜美代展、川村直子展 美的な衝撃に満ちた空間」『毎日新聞』、2001年10月9日夕刊
芥川喜好「芥川記者の展覧会へ行こう 9人が引き出す土の力」『読売新聞』、2003年10月18日夕刊
岸桂子「ギャラリー 大地の芸術 クレイワーク新世紀 『古い』素材に新たな命」『毎日新聞』、2003年10月22日夕刊
富田律之「かんさい21 9作家のクレイワーク展 土と向き合い土と戯れ」『日本経済新聞』、2003年10月23日夕刊
木村未来「美術 造形を見つけ出す展示 大阪と神戸で」『読売新聞』、2003年11月11日夕刊
兼吉毅「芸術に浸る 滋賀で『迫力の時代』展 大きな陶芸作品一堂に」『日本経済新聞』、2005年7月28日夕刊
「現代美術の謎を解き明かそう」『読売新聞』、2006年4月27日
小林哲夫「陶芸展―本物と見まがう作品 多治見・県現代陶芸美術館で『リアル～』はじまる」『毎日新聞』、2006年4月27日
「『陶芸の森』企画展 仏米巡回」『読売新聞』、2009年1月6日
芥川喜好「時の余白に ゴミの心に添うてみる」『読売新聞』、2016年5月28日
清水有香「美の庭―現代美術家 アンテナと好奇心で時代を成形」『毎日新聞』、2017年6月21日夕刊
正木利和「三島喜美代 神戸・ギャラリーヤマキファインアート」『産経新聞』、2017年9月22日夕刊
永田晶子「アートトピックス―『割れる新聞』つくる 三島喜美代さん 時代先取り50年」『毎日新聞』、2018年4月11日夕刊
尾島武子「アートリップ―今を映す巨大なくずかご」『朝日新聞』、2018年8月28日夕刊
「美と遊ぶ―三島喜美代『Works since the painting period: 1965-』ギャラリーヤマキファインアート」『産経新聞』、2018年9月14日夕刊
田中ゑれ奈「『割れるゴミ』創作 現代美術家が受賞―第5回安藤忠雄文化財団賞」『朝日新聞』、2019年5月21日夕刊
藤本幸太「間奏曲 ゴミがモチーフ 消費文化問う」『読売新聞』、2019年6月13日夕刊
清水有香「三島喜美代展 MEM」『毎日新聞』、2020年6月17日夕刊
高橋咲子「個展―三島喜美代が個展 東京・恵比寿」『毎日新聞』、2020年6月17日夕刊
田中ゑれ奈「87歳、ゴミで見せる現代社会」『朝日新聞』、2020年10月20日夕刊
正木利和「美と遊ぶ―三島喜美代展 ギャラリーヤマキファインアート」『産経新聞』、2020年10月23日夕刊
正木利和「一聞百見―三島喜美代さん（上）（中）（下）」『産経新聞』、2021年5月31日、6月1日、6月2日夕刊
大野択生「キャリア半世紀超 女性たちのエナジー」『朝日新聞』、2021年6月8日夕刊
「50年超独自創作 女性作家作品展」『読売新聞』、2021年6月10日
井上晋治「106歳から72歳 世界の女性作家16人 自らのアート信じた『エネルギー』」『読売新聞』、2021年9月2日
高橋咲子「アナザーエナジー展―美術界、多様性へ歩み ベテラン女性作家展／ジェンダー切り口話題」『毎日新聞』、2021年9月30日夕刊
建畠哲「気迫ある『命がけの遊び』第63回毎日芸術賞 受賞者の業績」『毎日新聞』、2022年1月1日
清水有香ほか「毎日芸術賞の人々―中 三島喜美代さん／下谷洋子さん」『毎日新聞』、2022年1月12日夕刊
「第63回毎日芸術賞：第63回毎日芸術賞贈呈式 受賞者喜びの声」『毎日新聞』、2022年2月9日夕刊
大堀瑠美「円空賞 県関係2氏」『岐阜新聞』、2023年2月1日
松崎晃子「ごみ題材に制作続ける90歳―三島喜美代さん」『中日新聞』、2023年2月4日夕刊
大堀瑠美「創造 ぎふ表現のいま―現代美術作家 三島喜美代さん」『岐阜新聞』、2023年2月25日
淵上えり子「100年LIFE―現代美術家 80歳代で脚光」『読売新聞』、2023年3月2日夕刊
清水有香「Topics―三島喜美代さん、京都で対談イベント『毎日失敗、面白い』90歳美術家の『人生訓』」『毎日新聞』、2023年4月24日夕刊
美間実沙「美術人ナビ @岐阜県現代陶芸美術館―割れる陶器で情報の危うさ」『読売新聞』、2023年10月30日朝刊
神宮桃子「情報・時代・私の交差点―福田美蘭 @名古屋・三島喜美代@岐阜」『朝日新聞』、2023年10月31日夕刊
山田夢留「ART―創作70年 三島喜美代展 岐阜・多治見 理屈なし、圧巻『ゴミ』遊び」『毎日新聞』、2023年11月13日夕刊

映像

「三島喜美代―人と作品―」岐阜県現代陶芸美術館、2005年（岐阜県現代陶芸美術館オリジナルビデオソフト）
「三島喜美代 命がけで遊ぶ」『日曜美術館』NHK Eテレ、2021年6月27日本放送、2021年7月4日再放送
「アートワールド―たぶん、すばらしき芸術の世界―」BSフジ、2021年11月20日、2021年11月29日放送
「デジタルミュージアム―清らなる工芸」HAB北陸朝日放送、2023年3月27日放送
「三島喜美代インタビュー」岐阜県現代陶芸美術館、2023年（三島喜美代―遊ぶ 見つめる 創りだす展）
ART360°（公益財団法人西枝財団）「三島喜美代―遊ぶ 見つめる 創りだす」https://art360.place/exhibitions/mishima-kimiyo-play-watch-create/（2024年3月20日、最終アクセス）

パブリックコレクション

（五十音順）

国内所蔵先

芦屋市立美術博物館
伊勢現代美術館
いわき市立美術館
大分県立美術館（利岡コレクション）
大原美術館
香美市立美術館
岐阜県現代陶芸美術館
京都国立近代美術館
京都市京セラ美術館
国際交流基金
国立工芸館
国立国際美術館
埼玉県桶川市（桶川駅西口公園）
札幌宮の森美術館
滋賀県立陶芸の森 陶芸館
太陽の森 ディマシオ美術館
高松市美術館
東京都現代美術館
岐阜県土岐市（東濃中部医療センター土岐市立総合病院）
栃木県立美術館
HAT神戸（灘の浜ファニチャーアート）
浜田市世界こども美術館
原美術館ARC
兵庫県立美術館
兵庫陶芸美術館
ベネッセアートサイト直島
北海道立近代美術館
北海道立函館美術館
ポーラ美術館
松本市美術館
森美術館
山口県立萩美術館・浦上記念館
和歌山県立近代美術館

海外所蔵先

アジアン・カルチュラル・カウンシル（ニューヨーク）
アリアナ美術館（ジュネーヴ）
アルコ美術館（旧韓国文化芸術振興院 美術会館）（ソウル）
ウスター美術館
ヴェフビ・コチ財団（イスタンブール）
エヴァーソン美術館（シラキュース）
M+（香港）
苑陶楽（北京）
オロット美術館
クイーンズランド・アートギャラリー（サウス・ブリスベン）
群山国立大学附設現代美術館
ケラミオン現代陶芸美術館（フレッヒェン）
国際陶芸スタジオ（ケチケメート）
国立台湾歴史博物館（台南）
シカゴ大学ブース・スクール・オブ・ビジネス
シカゴ美術館
シュピーツ芸術協会
ジョスリン美術館（オマハ）
スミス大学附属美術館（ノーサンプトン）
大英博物館（ロンドン）
パリ市立チェルヌスキ美術館
パリ市立近代美術館
ファエンツァ国際陶芸博物館
ファースト・ナショナルバンク・オブ・シカゴ
フロリダ大学サミュエル・P・ハーン美術館（ゲインズビル）
ボストン美術館
ポンピドゥー・センター／パリ国立近代美術館
南オーストラリア美術館（アデレード）
ミネアポリス美術館
ロサンゼルス・カウンティ美術館
ローマ日本文化会館

Public Collections

(in alphabetical order)

Japan

Ashiya City Museum of Art and History
Benesse Art Site Naoshima
Contemporary Art Museum ISE
Di-Maccio Art Museum, The Forest of Taiyo
Hagi Uragami Museum
Hakodate Museum of Art, Hokkaido
Hamada Children's Museum of Art
Hara Museum ARC
HAT Kobe (Furniture Art of Noda Beach)
Hokkaido Museum of Modern Art
Hyogo Prefectural Museum of Art
Iwaki City Art Museum
The Japan Foundation, Tokyo
Kami City Art Museum
Kyoto City KYOCERA Museum of Art
Matsumoto City Museum of Art
Miyanomori International Museum of Art, Sapporo
Mori Art Museum
The Museum of Ceramic Art, Hyogo
Museum of Contemporary Art Tokyo
The Museum of Modern Art, Wakayama
Museum of Modern Ceramic Art, Gifu
The National Crafts Museum
The National Museum of Art, Osaka
The National Museum of Modern Art, Kyoto
Ohara Museum of Art
Oita Prefectural Art Museum
Okegawa City Park, Saitama
Pola Museum of Art, Pola Art Foundation
The Shigaraki Ceramic Cultural Park, The Museum of Contemporary Ceramic Art
Takamatsu Art Museum
Tochigi Prefectural Museum of Fine Arts
Toki City, Gifu (Toki Municipal General Hospital)

Overseas

Ariana Museum, Geneva
ARKO Art Center, Soul (former Arts Councils Korea)
The Art Gallery of South Australia, Adelaide
The Art Institute of Chicago
The Asian Cultural Council, New York
The British Museum, London
Centre Pompidou / Musée national d'art moderne, Paris
Cernuschi Museum, Paris
The Everson Museum of Art, Syracuse
First National Bank of Chicago
Hap Pottery, Beijing
International Ceramics Studio, Kecskemét
Istituto Giapponese di Cultura in Roma
Joslyn Art Museum, Omaha
Keramion, Frechen
Kunsan National University Museum
Kunst Gesellschaft Spiez
Los Angeles County Museum of Art
The Minneapolis Institute of Art
Museo Internazionale delle Ceramiche in Faenza
Musée d'art moderne de la Ville de Paris
Museum of Fine Arts, Boston
The Museum of Art Olot
M+, Hong Kong
National Museum of Taiwan History, Tainan
Queensland Art gallery, South Brisbane
Samuel P. Harn Museum of Art, Gainesville
Smith College, Northampton
The University of Chicago Booth School of Business
Vebi Koc Foundation ARTER, Istanbul
Worceter Art Museum

作品リスト
List of Works

No.	作品名 Title	制作年 Year	素材、技法 Material, Technique	寸法(H × W × Dcm) Dimensions	所蔵 Collection
1	マスカット *Muscats*	1951年	油彩、カンヴァス Oil on canvas	61.0×73.0 cm	個人蔵 Private Collection
2	かぼちゃ *Pumpkin*	1952年	油彩、カンヴァス Oil on canvas	91.0×73.0 cm	個人蔵 Private Collection
3	作品B *Work B*	1952年	油彩、カンヴァス Oil on canvas	73.0×91.0 cm	個人蔵 Private Collection
4	スケッチカード *Sketch Cards*	1957年	素描、紙(24点) Drawing on paper (24 sheet)	13.0×10.0 cm	個人蔵 Private Collection
5-1	Untitled	1957年	素描、紙 Drawing on paper	54.0×38.0cm	個人蔵 Private Collection
5-2	Untitled	1957年	素描、紙 Drawing on paper	54.0×38.0cm	個人蔵 Private Collection
6	スケッチブック *Sketchbook*	1957年	素描、紙 Drawing on paper	36.0×26.0 cm	個人蔵 Private Collection
7	覇 *Ascendancy*	1960年	油彩、カンヴァス Oil on canvas	130.0×162.0 cm	個人蔵 Private Collection
8	Work 60-B	1960年	新聞、雑誌、ポスター、油彩、合板 Oil on plywood, newspaper, magazines, poster	130.0×92.0 cm	美術資料センター株式会社 Bijutsu Shiryo Center Co., Ltd.
9	Work-64-I	1964年	新聞、雑誌、油彩、板 Oil on board, newspaper, magazines	183.0×123.0 cm	京都国立近代美術館 The National Museum of Modern Art, Kyoto
10	Work 64-III	1964年	新聞、雑誌、包装紙、油彩、合板 Oil on plywood, newspaper, magazines, wrapping paper	183.0×123.0 cm	個人蔵 Private Collection
11	作品 65-H *Work 65-H*	1965年	新聞、雑誌、油彩、合板 Oil on plywood, newspaper, magazines	183.0×137.5 cm	個人蔵 Private Collection
12	変貌 III *Transfiguration III*	1966年	新聞、雑誌、ポスター、油彩、カンヴァス Oil on canavs, newspaper, magazines, poster	162.0×130.5 cm	美術資料センター株式会社 Bijutsu Shiryo Center Co., Ltd.
13	断章 III *Morceau III*	1966年	新聞、雑誌、油彩、カンヴァス Oil on canvas, newspaper, magazines	162.0×131.0 cm	京都国立近代美術館 The National Museum of Modern Art, Kyoto
14	ヴィーナスの変貌 V *Transfiguration of Venus V*	1967年	新聞、アクリル絵具、シルクスクリーン、合板 Acrylic on plywood, newspaper, silkscreen	180.0×180.0 cm	個人蔵 Private Collection
15	作品 68-A *Work 68-A*	1968年	油彩、カンヴァス Oil on canvas	181.0×223.0 cm	個人蔵 Private Collection
16	作品F *Work F*	1969年	雑誌、油彩、カンヴァス Oil on canvas, magazines	130.0×162.0 cm	個人蔵 Private Collection
17	Untitled	1970年	アクリル絵具、シルクスクリーン、カンヴァス Acrylic on canvas, silkscreen	130.0×162.0 cm	個人蔵 Private Collection

No.	作品名 Title	制作年 Year	素材、技法 Material, Technique	寸法(H×W×Dcm) Dimensions	所蔵 Collection
18	Untitled	1970-71年	アクリル絵具、 シルクスクリーン、カンヴァス Acrylic on canvas, silkscreen	130.0×162.0 cm	個人蔵 Private Collection
19	メモリー III *Memory III*	1971年	馬券、油彩、カンヴァス Oil on canvas, horse racing ticket	162.0×130.0 cm	個人蔵 Private Collection
20-1	Paper Bag E-1	1973年	陶、転写 Silkscreen on ceramic	47.9×30.6×34.4 cm	兵庫陶芸美術館 The Museum of Ceramic Art, Hyogo
20-2	Paper Bag E-5	1973年	陶、転写 Silkscreen on ceramic	48.4×35.5×26.8 cm	兵庫陶芸美術館 The Museum of Ceramic Art, Hyogo
20-3	Paper Bag E-6	1974年	陶、転写 Silkscreen on ceramic	45.0×38.0×30.0 cm	兵庫陶芸美術館 The Museum of Ceramic Art, Hyogo
20-4	Paper Bag E-S1	1977年	陶、転写 Silkscreen on ceramic	33.0×22.0×18.0 cm	兵庫陶芸美術館 The Museum of Ceramic Art, Hyogo
20-5	Paper Bag E-S2	1977年	陶、転写 Silkscreen on ceramic	32.0×23.0×19.0 cm	兵庫陶芸美術館 The Museum of Ceramic Art, Hyogo
20-6	Paper Bag E-S3	1977年	陶、転写 Silkscreen on ceramic	31.0×23.0×20.0 cm	兵庫陶芸美術館 The Museum of Ceramic Art, Hyogo
20-7	Paper Bag E-S4	1977年	陶、転写 Silkscreen on ceramic	32.0×24.0×20.0 cm	兵庫陶芸美術館 The Museum of Ceramic Art, Hyogo
20-8	Paper Bag E-7	1980年	陶、転写 Silkscreen on ceramic	37.0×39.0×29.0 cm	兵庫陶芸美術館 The Museum of Ceramic Art, Hyogo
21	D-1	1973年	陶、転写 Silkscreen on ceramic	10.0×37.5×34.0 cm	個人蔵 Private Collection
22	Package '74	1973-74年	陶、転写、彩色 Silkscreen and hand-painted on ceramic	サイズ可変 Dimension variable	滋賀県立陶芸の森 陶芸館 The Shigaraki Ceramic Cultural Park, The Museum of Contemporary Ceramic Art
23	Untitled	1975年	陶、転写 Silkscreen on ceramic	16.0×31.0×14.0 cm	個人蔵 Private Collection
24	Untitled	1975年	陶、転写 Silkscreen on ceramic	29.0×34.5×12.5 cm	個人蔵 Private Collection
25	Untitled	1975年	陶、転写 Silkscreen on ceramic	31.0×40.0×25.0 cm	個人蔵 Private Collection
26	Untitled	1975年	陶、転写 Silkscreen on ceramic	37.5×34.0×19.0 cm	個人蔵 Private Collection
27	Untitled	1975年	陶、転写 Silkscreen on ceramic	21.0×39.0×13.0 cm	個人蔵 Private Collection

No.	作品名 Title	制作年 Year	素材、技法 Material, Technique	寸法（H×W×Dcm） Dimensions	所蔵 Collection
28	Untitled	1975年	陶、転写 Silkscreen on ceramic	28.5×30.0×12.0 cm	個人蔵 Private Collection
29	Untitled	1975年	陶、転写 Silkscreen on ceramic	21.0×32.0×13.0 cm	個人蔵 Private Collection
30	Film 75	1975年	陶、転写 Silkscreen on ceramic	60.0×180.0×50.0 cm	個人蔵 Private Collection
31	Newspaper 76	1976年	陶、転写 Silkscreen on ceramic	9.5×23.0×18.0 cm	個人蔵 Private Collection
32	Newspaper 76	1976年	陶、転写 Silkscreen on ceramic	8.0×22.0×18.0 cm	個人蔵 Private Collection
33	Copy 76	1976年	陶、転写 Silkscreen on ceramic	15.0×23.5 cm	個人蔵 Private Collection
34	Copy 76	1976年	陶、転写 Silkscreen on ceramic	1.0×16.0×18.0 cm	個人蔵 Private Collection
35	Copy 78	1978年	陶、転写 Silkscreen on ceramic	30.0×22.0 cm	個人蔵 Private Collection
36	球 Copy-78-A4 *Ball: Copy-78-A4*	1978年	陶、転写 Silkscreen on ceramic	11.0×12.0×11.0 cm	個人蔵 Private Collection
37	球 Copy-78-A5 *Ball: Copy-78-A5*	1978年	陶、転写 Silkscreen on ceramic	22.0×23.0×22.0 cm	個人蔵 Private Collection
38	Package '78	1978年	陶、転写、彩色 Silkscreen and hand-painted on ceramic	Cal Fame Lemon/ Newspapers：50.0×47.0×37.0 cm Coca Cola Bottle & Box：22.0×6.0、9.5×27.5×22.5 cm Coca Cola Box：18.9×45.0×30.5 cm Kochi：23.5×31.5×27.0 cm	滋賀県立陶芸の森 陶芸館 The Shigaraki Ceramic Cultural Park, The Museum of Contemporary Ceramic Art
39	Notebook 80	1980年	陶、転写 Silkscreen on ceramic	0.5×28.0×19.5 cm	個人蔵 Private Collection
40	Comic Book '80	1980年	陶、転写、彩色 Silkscreen and hand-painted on ceramic	積本：28.0×24.0×28.5 cm、伏せ本：11.3×37.5×28.0 cm	滋賀県立陶芸の森 陶芸館 The Shigaraki Ceramic Cultural Park, The Museum of Contemporary Ceramic Art
41	Untitled	1981年	エッチング、紙 Etching on paper	45.7×31.1 cm	個人蔵 Private Collection
42	Untitled	1981年	エッチング、紙 Etching on paper	31.1×45.5 cm	個人蔵 Private Collection
43	Untitled	1981年	エッチング、紙 Etching on paper	31.1×45.5 cm	個人蔵 Private Collection
44	Untitled	1981年	エッチング、紙 Etching on paper	31.1×45.5 cm	個人蔵 Private Collection
45	Untitled	1981年	エッチング、紙 Etching on paper	45.5×31.2 cm	個人蔵 Private Collection

No.	作品名 Title	制作年 Year	素材、技法 Material, Technique	寸法(H×W×Dcm) Dimensions	所蔵 Collection
46	Newspaper 83	1983年	陶、転写 Silkscreen on ceramic	26.0×11.0×10.5 cm	個人蔵 Private Collection
47	Untitled	1984年	陶、転写 Silkscreen on ceramic	51.0×115.0×73.0 cm	個人蔵 Private Collection
48	Untitled	1984年	陶、転写 Silkscreen on ceramic	38.0×90.0×63.5 cm	個人蔵 Private Collection
49	Column-2	1984-85年	陶、転写、彩色、コンクリート、鉄 Silkscreen and hand-painted on ceramic, concrete, iron	135.0×100.0×98.0 cm	滋賀県立陶芸の森 陶芸館 The Shigaraki Ceramic Cultural Park, The Museum of Contemporary Ceramic Art
50	閉じ込められた情報B *Confined Information B*	1989年	陶、転写、コンクリート、鉄 Silkscreen on ceramic, concrete, iron	150.0×60.0×60.0 cm	個人蔵 Private Collection
51	閉じ込められた情報C *Confined Information C*	1989年	陶、転写、コンクリート、鉄 Silkscreen on ceramic, concrete, iron	150.0×60.0×60.0 cm	個人蔵 Private Collection
52	Untitled	1990年	陶、転写、彩色 Silkscreen and hand-painted on ceramic	21.0×46.0×45.0 cm	個人蔵 Private Collection
53	FOCUS 91	1991年	陶、転写、彩色 Silkscreen and hand-painted on ceramic	8.5×38.0×32.0 cm	個人蔵 Private Collection
54	WORK C-92	1991-92年	陶、転写、彩色 Silkscreen and hand-painted on ceramic	110.0×165.0×86.0 cm	岐阜県現代陶芸美術館 Museum of Modern Ceramic Art, Gifu
55	サンキスボックス *Sunkis Box*	2005年	陶、転写、彩色 Silkscreen and hand-painted on ceramic	39.0×54.0×39.0 cm	岐阜県現代陶芸美術館 Museum of Modern Ceramic Art, Gifu
56	バナナボックス *Banana Box*	2007年	陶、転写、彩色 Silkscreen and hand-painted on ceramic	20.5×32.0×48.0 cm	岐阜県現代陶芸美術館 Museum of Modern Ceramic Art, Gifu
57	楽譜 *Musical Score*	2007年	陶、転写 Silkscreen on ceramic	10.0×48.0×25.0 cm	岐阜県現代陶芸美術館 Museum of Modern Ceramic Art, Gifu
58-1	リーフレット(赤) *Leaflet [Red]*	2007-08年	陶、転写、彩色(11枚) Silkscreen and hand-painted on ceramic (11 sheet)	40.0×29.0 cm	岐阜県現代陶芸美術館 Museum of Modern Ceramic Art, Gifu
58-2	リーフレット(青) *Leaflet [Blue]*	2007-08年	陶、転写、彩色(9枚) Silkscreen and hand-painted on ceramic (9 sheet)	40.0×29.0 cm	岐阜県現代陶芸美術館 Museum of Modern Ceramic Art, Gifu
59	KOUKOKU 08	2008年	陶、転写、彩色 Silkscreen and hand-painted on ceramic	7.0×34.0×25.0 cm	個人蔵 Private Collection
60	KOUKOKU 08	2008年	陶、転写、彩色 Silkscreen and hand-painted on ceramic	22.0×31.0 cm	個人蔵 Private Collection

No.	作品名 Title	制作年 Year	素材、技法 Material, Technique	寸法(H × W × Dcm) Dimensions	所蔵 Collection
61	KOUKOKU 08	2008年	陶、転写、彩色 Silkscreen and hand-painted on ceramic	6.0×37.0×26.0 cm	個人蔵 Private Collection
62	KOUKOKU 08	2008年	陶、転写、彩色 Silkscreen and hand-painted on ceramic	7.0×22.0×30.0 cm	個人蔵 Private Collection
63	KOUKOKU 08	2008年	陶、転写、彩色 Silkscreen and hand-painted on ceramic	37.0×14.0 cm	個人蔵 Private Collection
64	KOUKOKU 08	2008年	陶、転写、彩色 Silkscreen and hand-painted on ceramic	35.5×26.0 cm	個人蔵 Private Collection
65	Box Orange 19	2019年	陶、転写、彩色 Silkscreen and hand-painted on ceramic	39.0×43.5×33.0 cm	個人蔵 Private Collection
66	Work 20-T	2020年	陶、転写、彩色、ワイヤー、紙、新聞、紐、ビニール Silkscreen and hand-painted on ceramic, wire, paper, newspaper, string, vinyl	左:46.0×43.0×29.0 cm 右:61.0×42.0×29.0 cm	個人蔵 Private Collection
67	Work 22-Sunkist 2	2022年	陶、転写、彩色 Silkscreen and hand-painted on ceramic	39.0×46.0×24.0 cm	個人蔵 Private Collection
68	Work 23-TAG	2023年	陶、転写、彩色、ワイヤー(10枚) Silkscreen and hand-painted on ceramic, wire (10 sheet)	30.0×15.0 cm	個人蔵 Private Collection
69	Work 86-B	1987年	ポリエチレン、転写、鉄、木、ワイヤー Silkscreen on polyethylene, iron, wood, wire	65.0×24.0×23.0 cm	個人蔵 Private Collection
70	Work 90-BG	1990年	陶、転写、彩色、木 Silkscreen and hand-painted on ceramic, wood	29.0×28.0×28.0 cm	個人蔵 Private Collection
71	Work 92-N1	1992年	陶、転写、ブリキ缶 Silkscreen on ceramic, tin can	41.0×22.5×29.0 cm	個人蔵 Private Collection
72	Work 92-N2	1992年	陶、転写、ブリキ缶 Silkscreen on ceramic, tin can	27.0×20.0×18.0 cm	個人蔵 Private Collection
73	Comic Book 03-1	2003年	溶融スラグ、転写、彩色 Silkscreen and hand-painted on melted slag	34.0×123.0×92.0 cm	ポーラ美術館 Pola Museum of Art
74	Comic Book 03-2	2003年	溶融スラグ、転写、彩色 Silkscreen and hand-painted on melted slag	35.0×126.0×91.0 cm	ポーラ美術館 Pola Museum of Art
75	Comic Book 03-3	2003年	溶融スラグ、転写、彩色 Silkscreen and hand-painted on melted slag	35.0×134.0×93.0 cm	個人蔵 Private Collection

No.	作品名 Title	制作年 Year	素材、技法 Material, Technique	寸法（H × W × Dcm） Dimensions	所蔵 Collection
76	Work 17-POT	2017年	陶、転写、彩色 Silkscreen and hand-painted on ceramic	25.0×25.0×25.0 cm	個人蔵 Private Collection
77	Work 17-C	2017年	陶、転写、彩色、鉄 Silkscreen and hand-painted on ceramic, iron	74.0×64.0×64.0 cm	ポーラ美術館 Pola Museum of Art
78	Work 21-B	2021年	鉄、木、シラス（火山灰） Iron, wood, shirasu (volcanic ashes)	67.0×51.0×60.0 cm	個人蔵 Private Collection
79	Work 21-G	2021年	陶、転写、彩色、鉄 Silkscreen and hand-painted on ceramic, iron	105.0×68.0×62.0 cm	個人蔵 Private Collection
80	Work 21-C2	2021年	陶、転写、彩色、鉄 Silkscreen and hand-painted on ceramic, iron	79.0×55.0×55.0 cm	個人蔵 Private Collection
81	Work 22-P	2022年	陶、転写、鉄、アルミ、木、ポリプロピレン Silkscreen on ceramic, iron, aluminium, wood, polypropylene	117.0×231.0×236.0 cm	個人蔵 Private Collection
82	20世紀の記憶 *Memories of the 20th Century*	1984-2013年	耐火レンガに転写（1万600個） Silkscreen on old firebricks (10,600 pieces)	サイズ可変 Dimension variable	個人蔵 Private Collection
83	化石になった情報 88 *Fossilized Information 88*	1986-88年	陶、転写、鉄、木、車輪付きメタルシェルフ Silkscreen on ceramic, iron, wood, wheeled metal shelf	170.0×142.0×70.0 cm	個人蔵 Private Collection

参考出品
Reference exhibits

—	空き缶 Empty cans	——	——	——	個人蔵 Private Collection
—	溶融スラグ Melted slag	——	——	——	個人蔵 Private Collection
—	資料一式 Documents	——	——	——	個人蔵 Private Collection

写真クレジット
Photography Credits

撮影 | Photo Credits

宮川邦雄　nos. 1~4, 5-1, 6, 7, 10, 14~16, 18, 19, 21, 31~35, 39, 41~48, 52~63, 66, 68, 71, 72, 76, 78, fig. 10, 11, 13, 18, カバー裏

小川重雄　nos. 8, 11, 12, 50, 51, 70, 82, 83, fig. 4, 6, 7, p. 4, 41,

竹見良二　nos. 5-2, 17, 23~29, 36, 37, 64, 65, 67, 81

加藤成文　nos. 20-1~20-8

杉本賢正　nos. 22, 38, 40, 49

中川忠明　nos. 30, 77, カバー表

今村裕司　nos. 73~75, p. 184

古川裕也　nos. 79, 80, fig. 17

木暮伸也　fig. 1

Alice H. North.　fig. 14

写真提供 | Photo Courtesy

岐阜県現代陶芸美術館　nos. 1~4, 5-1, 6, 7, 10, 14~19, 21, 31~35, 39, 41~48, 52~63, 66, 68, 71, 72, 76, 78, fig. 10, 11, 13, 18, カバー裏

美術資料センター株式会社　nos. 8, 11, 12, 50, 51, 70, 82, 83, fig. 4, 6, 7, p. 4, 41

京都国立近代美術館　nos. 9, 13

兵庫陶芸美術館　nos. 20-1~20-8

滋賀県立陶芸の森 陶芸館　nos. 22, 38, 40, 49

艸居　nos. 30, 73~75, 77, fig. 12, p. 184, カバー表

MEM　図1, no. 69

東京都現代美術館　図2

森美術館　nos. 79, 80, fig. 17

公益財団法人アルカンシエール美術財団／原美術館コレクション　fig. 1

太陽の森 ディマシオ美術館　fig. 2

美濃陶磁歴史館　fig. 3

大原美術館　fig. 5

三島喜美代・上田準三　figs. 8, 9, 12, 15, pp. 178-183, 222

ベネッセハウス　fig. 14

ART FACTORY 城南島　fig. 16

謝辞

本展覧会の開催ならびに本書の刊行にあたりまして、多大なご協力を賜りました三島喜美代様、ご家族の皆様をはじめ、貴重な作品や資料を快くご出品くださった美術館、ご所蔵家の方々、そして様々な面でご協力いただきました関係者の皆様方に、厚く御礼申し上げます。

(五十音順・敬称略)

ART FACTORY 城南島
MEM
大原美術館
株式会社ギャラリー1045
株式会社東横イン
岐阜県現代陶芸美術館
京都国立近代美術館
滋賀県立陶芸の森 陶芸館
艸居
太陽の森 ディマシオ美術館
東京都現代美術館
土岐市美濃陶磁歴史館
原美術館ARC
美術資料センター株式会社
兵庫陶芸美術館
ベネッセアートサイト直島
公益財団法人ポーラ美術振興財団 ポーラ美術館
森美術館

三島喜美代

上田準三
吉田文雄

秋元雄史
石﨑泰之
岩﨑余帆子
岡田享子
金子美環
島敦彦
菅原彩加
杉山昌平
鈴木郷史
高橋瑞穂
高村惠利
建畠晢
谷本晃一
西田麗菜
花井素子
日埜直彦
福永治
藤田篤実
保坂健二朗
鈎真一
牧口千夏
牧瀬浩一
牧野健太郎
松原龍一
水嶋恵理
水嶋龍一郎
山塙菜未

Acknowledgments

We would like to express our deep gratitude to Mishima Kimiyo and her family for their considerable support, as well as to all museums, companies and private owners who willingly provided items from their valuable collections, and to everyone else who contributed in one way or another to the realization of this exhibition and the publication of this catalogue.

(alphabetical order・honorific title)

ART FACTORY JONANJIMA
Benesse Art Site Naoshima
Bijutsu Shiryo Center Co., Ltd.
Di-Maccio Art Museum, The Forest of Taiyo
Gallery 1045 Co., Ltd.
Hara Museum ARC
MEM
Mori Art Museum
The Museum of Ceramic Art, Hyogo
Museum of Contemporary Art Tokyo
Museum of Modern Ceramic Art, Gifu
The National Museum of Modern Art, Kyoto
Ohara Museum of Art
Pola Museum of Art, Pola Art Foundation
The Shigaraki Ceramic Cultural Park, The Museum of Contemporary Ceramic Art
Sokyo Gallery
Toki City Historical Museum of Mino Ceramics
Toyoko INN Co., Ltd.

Mishima Kimiyo

Ueda Junzo
Yoshida Fumio

Akimoto Yuji
Fujita Atsumi
Fukunaga Osamu
Hanai Motoko
Hino Naohiko
Hosaka Kenjiro
Ishizaki Yasuyuki
Iwasaki Yoko
Kaneko Miwa
Magari Shinichi
Makiguchi Chinatsu
Makino Kentaro
Makise Kouichi
Matsubara Ryuichi
Mizushima Eri
Mizushima Ryuichiro
Nishida Reina
Okada Kyoko
Shima Atsuhiko
Sugawara Ayaka
Sugiyama Ryohei
Suzuki Satoshi
Takahashi Mizuho
Takamura Eri
Tanimoto Koichi
Tatehata Akira
Yamabana Nami

本書は「三島喜美代―未来への記憶」展の公式図録として刊行されました。

This book was published as the official catalogue of the "Mishima Kimiyo: Memories for the Future" exhibition.

三島喜美代―未来への記憶

Mishima Kimiyo: Memories for the Future

練馬区立美術館
2024年5月19日(日)～7月7日(日)

Nerima Art Museum, Tokyo
May 19-July 7, 2024

[展覧会]

主催
練馬区立美術館(公益財団法人練馬区文化振興協会)

協力
株式会社東横イン／株式会社ギャラリー1045

企画・構成
伊東正伸(練馬区立美術館 館長)

企画協力
上田準三

学芸担当
小野寛子、新井晃(練馬区立美術館学芸員)

広報・管理担当
梅津光(練馬区立美術館)

広報物デザイン
川添英昭

[Exhibition]

Organized by
Nerima Art Museum/Nerima Cultural Promotion Association

In Cooperation with
Toyoko Inn Co., Ltd./Gallery 1045 Co., Ltd.

Planned by
Ito Masanobu (Director, Nerima Art Museum)

Supervised by
Ueda Junzo

Curated by
Ono Hiroko, Arai Hikaru (Curators of Nerima Art Museum)

Coordinated by
Umetsu Hikaru (Nerima Art Museum)

Publicity Design
Kawazoe Hideaki

[カタログ]

執筆
徳山拓一(森美術館 アソシエイト・キュレーター)
森村泰昌(美術家)
伊東正伸
新井晃

翻訳
クリストファー・スティヴンズ
アンドレアス・シュトゥールマン

企画・編集
練馬区立美術館

ブックデザイン
川添英昭

編集協力
福岡優子(青幻舎)
久下まり子(青幻舎)

[Catalogue]

Texts
Tokuyama Hirokazu (Associate Curator, Mori Art Museum)
Morimura Yasumasa (Artist)
Ito Masanobu
Arai Hikaru

Translation
Christopher Stephens
Andreas Stuhlmann

Concept, Editing
Nerima Art Museum

Book Design
Kawazoe Hideaki

Co-editing
Fukuoka Yuko (Seigensha)
Kuge Mariko (Seigensha)

三島喜美代 —未来への記憶

2024年5月30日　初版発行

編集
練馬区立美術館

発行者
片山誠

発行所
株式会社青幻舎
京都市中京区梅忠町9–1　〒604-8136
Tel. 075–252–6766 Fax. 075–252–6770
https://www.seigensha.com

印刷・製本
株式会社山田写真製版所

ISBN978-4-86152-956-6 C0070

Mishima Kimiyo: Memories for the Future

First edition May 30, 2024

Edited by
Nerima Art Museum

Publisher
Katayama Makoto

Published by
Seigensha Art Publishing, Inc.
9-1, Umetada-cho, Nakagyo-ku, Kyoto, 604-8136, Japan
Tel. +81-75-252-6766 Fax. +81-75-252-6770
https://www.seigensha.com

Printed and Bound by
Yamada Photo Process Co., Ltd.

ISBN978-4-86152-956-6 C0070